REBOOT

REBOOT

PROBABLY MORE THAN YOU EVER WANTED TO KNOW ABOUT STARTING A GLOBAL BUSINESS

JODIE FOX

CO-FOUNDER OF SHOES OF PREY

WILEY

First published in 2020 by John Wiley & Sons Australia, Ltd
42 McDougall St, Milton Qld 4064

Office also in Melbourne

Typeset in Alegreya Medium 11/14pt

© John Wiley & Sons Australia, Ltd 2020

The moral rights of the author have been asserted

ISBN: 978-0-730-34943-3

A catalogue record for this book is available from the National Library of Australia

Cover design by Wiley

Back cover image © Shoes of Prey Inc.

Internal background image: © Ursula Alter / Getty Images

10 9 8 7 6 5 4 3 2 1

Disclaimer
The material in this publication is of the nature of general comment only, and does not represent professional advice. It is not intended to provide specific guidance for particular circumstances and it should not be relied on as the basis for any decision to take action or not take action on any matter which it covers. Readers should obtain professional advice where appropriate, before making any such decision. To the maximum extent permitted by law, the author and publisher disclaim all responsibility and liability to any person, arising directly or indirectly from any person taking or not taking action based on the information in this publication.

CONTENTS

FOREWORD

Everyone has faced a moment in which they had absolutely no idea what to do. Perhaps they were confronted with a blank page. A cliff to jump off or a ladder to slowly climb down. An unknown path or a known path. Maybe they received lots of advice about which option to choose. Maybe they studied other people who had faced similar circumstances. Ultimately, though—they were alone. Because the only person who can make a decision for you is YOU.

These intersections are lonely places. If anyone does offer advice, it often sounds something like 'just make a decision'. In these situations, without an immediate, clear answer, we feel weak and incompetent. We think everyone else has it figured out. But the more open we are about the logical and emotional process of decision making, the more we realise this experience is normal and surmountable. This gives us courage, and the more prepared we are to make decisions for ourselves when there is no map.

* * *

I remember facing my first major decision without a map. I was 17 years old and I was finishing up my high school exams. I was sitting on the kitchen floor with a book that listed every Australian university course offered. Essentially, I was supposed to find what I would do for the rest of my life in this book. Dancer, lawyer, industrial engineer? And what did that mean anyway? Little did I know that this was my first step on an entirely unmapped path. I had talked to career counsellors. I did work experience. Yet for the first time, no-one knew better than I did.

This experience was a daily occurrence for me in building Shoes of Prey.

Shoes of Prey grew from an idea dreamed up over a lazy afternoon at the beach to a business with over US$27 million in funding, shipping to over 100 countries every single month, completely reinventing the supply chain for footwear, and, at its peak, employing a team of 220 across four countries.

It ended with me alone, at risk of kidnapping, navigating the demands of stakeholders and public scrutiny while unsalaried, burnt out and blindsided with the most unmappable decisions imaginable, multiple times a day, every day, for months and months on end.

But I didn't break. I found my core values. I found my identity. And I chose to reboot and try again every single day.

Most stories of entrepreneur and business successes are reflections with 20/20 hindsight and rose-coloured glasses. They're written when success is a sure thing, when every decision, it turns out, was the right one. Or, if not, a perfect lesson that leads to ultimate success.

I think that would be an interesting book. But I don't think it's actually that helpful. And, Shoes of Prey was not that business. It didn't work out.

This book shares what it *felt* like at ground zero. Which is probably more than you wanted to know about starting global business. It shares the frameworks I worked out to make decisions rather than stagnate. I hope it will help you to feel both prepared and 'normal' when you inevitably hit these moments. Maybe it'll even help you to not make some of the poorer decisions I made along the way.

And, maybe, when you've read this book, you'll share with me and with others your experiences at your own unmappable moments, and we'll all get so much better (and feel less lonely) in these moments.

About the Author

Jodie Fox is an entrepreneur who may or may not make it.

Jodie Fox was a co-founder and the creative director of Shoes of Prey. A banking and finance lawyer by trade and a dedicated creative, Fox created a perfect nexus of the corporate and creative worlds when she co-founded Shoes of Prey.

Identifying and serving a gap in the market for custom-made shoes at non-luxury prices, Shoes of Prey was considered a global leader and innovator in mass-customisation and on-demand manufacturing. A vertically-integrated business that raised over US$27 million in funding, and with more than six million shoes designed, Shoes of Prey changed the way the retail industry thought about product and manufacturing.

Shoes of Prey ceased trading in August 2018. Now Jodie Fox is rebooting herself for her next venture.

In recognition of her work at Shoes of Prey, Fox was a judge at the World Retail Awards (2016, 2017, 2018) lectured the Stanford Graduate School of Business MBA Class (2016, 2017, 2018) and regularly keynotes events including the National Retail Federation conference (2017), Virgin Australia Melbourne Fashion Festival (alongside Renzo Rosso, Nicola Formichetti and Fern Mallis) and the American Apparel and Footwear Association Executive Summit (2016).

Accolades collected by Fox personally include:

- Two Ten Women In Footwear Industry Impact Awards — Inaugural WIFI Influencer Award (2018)

- listed as number 6 in the Top 50 Australian and New Zealand Women in Tech (2016)

- *Elle Magazine* Style Awards — Fashion Innovator of the Year, Australia (2015)

- Griffith University Business School Outstanding Alumni (2015)

- Top 30 most influential women in Australian retail (2014)

- Top 10 Australian female entrepreneurs (2014)

- finalist for the *InStyle* Audi Woman of Style Awards (2014)

- *Cosmopolitan Magazine*'s top 30 women (2013)

- Telstra Businesswoman of the Year (Australia) — Private & Corporate Sector (2011).

INTRODUCTION

Shoes of Prey was the place where women could design their own shoes. What started as an idea hatched by three friends became our full-time jobs, then a venture-backed company with over US$27 million in funding and a loyal global following.

Our energies were focused on building technology so that our shoe-loving customers would be able to create a shoe design, and see a photo-realistic version of it in real time, before clicking 'buy'.

Shoe-lovers could choose from so many options. Multiple heel heights, from flat all the way to six-inch heels. The heels could be stiletto, block or wedge heels. There were all the colours of the rainbow, in textiles or leather. Pointed toe, round toe, almond toe. Boots, sneakers, sandals, pumps, mules ... The list went on and the options were, for all intents and purposes, endless.

Throughout the lifetime of the business, the vast majority of our reasonably large audience came to us purely through word of mouth. Our Net Promoter Scores were through the roof, and we were scrappy and smart about building the business further.

When we didn't have a marketing budget for advertising, we were one of the first companies to work with social media influencers. Our earliest influencer campaign led to media coverage that permanently tripled our sales.

When there weren't any factories that could make one pair of shoes at a time on the scale that we needed (or rather, there weren't any factories that wanted to spend the time figuring it out), we were the first (to my knowledge) to build a factory dedicated to making one pair of shoes at a time, at scale.

Millions of shoes were designed on our site. The shoe industry, the retail industry and the fashion industry all hailed the concept as the future of buying shoes, and the business won countless awards. Top tier venture capitalists and retailers alike joined our investor syndicate. Yet ultimately, despite all of these incredibly-positive indicators, in the end, the mass market fit simply was not there.

Alongside this extraordinary business journey was the 'other' business journey that's rarely talked about. What the highs felt like. What the lows were really like. What standing on the precipice of a decision feels like, when there's no map and *only you* can make the decision. And, everyone is counting on you to make the right decision.

The 'other' business journey also covers when you realise you need to cease trading. What it feels like to fire 160 people by yourself. What it feels like to carry on with your day knowing you're at risk of being kidnapped. What happens when you divorce your co-founder.

And, how we all have the strength to pick ourselves up, day after day, rebooting each morning to do it all again.

Right now I'm rebooting my whole life. And this book is the turning point.

PHASE 1
ON LEARNING AND CHOOSING

Wisdom gathering: an emotional, intellectual and spiritual learning phase that's extremely uncomfortable and confronting. But entirely necessary to move forward and grow.

I think of the early stages of a journey as wisdom gathering. It's when we're learning and making choices. It's a time when you go through a series of really difficult experiences that teach you lessons that end up serving you. They're the price you must pay if you want to learn. I'm never comfortable in the moments of wisdom gathering. In fact, I find it unpleasant, dark and scary. Yet I almost always look back on them as the necessary and shining highlights of the journey.

CHAPTER 1
LEARNING BY DOING

It was 4 pm on a weekday afternoon and I was sitting on my parents' kitchen floor, surrounded by books, papers and guides to choosing my university degree. My close friend Fiona was leaning over the kitchen counter urging me to make a decision.

I had just 30 minutes to submit my final university preferences for what felt like the beginning of a very specific path I'd have to take for the rest of my life. I'd auditioned to get into a dance course and been told to simply put it as my first preference to get in. And that's what I'd selected. However, I also knew I would likely get a high school finishing score that would be good enough to get into a dual degree of law and international business. I was torn. And it was down to the wire.

The pressure around this decision was all of my own doing. My parents were the most supportive parents imaginable. Both had grown up in poor families descended from even poorer families. Each generation had dedicated their energy to building a better set of opportunities for their children, and particularly with respect to education.

My Nonna (my Italian grandmother) had reached a mid-primary school level of education in a rural town in Sicily. My perception of her mother is that she was a harsh woman who saw more value in my Nonna doing physical labour than in attending school. This was likely born of a situation in which labour supported the family financially, whereas school came at a cost.

My mother got to mid-high school, and my father got to complete high school. He had excellent grades but couldn't afford to put them to use by attending university. Both of my parents prized education highly and, as I was part of the first generation of the family able to choose a tertiary future, I felt both the weight of responsibility and the overwhelming feeling that comes with uncharted territory.

While my father didn't have practical advice for me on tertiary education, he had given me something arguably more valuable: he'd fostered in me an awe and excitement around the potential the world held. When I was little he continually encouraged me to keep speaking Italian with Mum—if I spoke two languages I could be a diplomat, or an international businessperson, he told me. He gently encouraged me to picture an adulthood of travelling and working in a high-flying executive role.

He may have got more than he bargained for. As a child I broke down in tears at the suggestion of leaving Lismore for university in Sydney, a 12-hour drive away, telling my dad I would never ever want to leave Lismore, because I would never *ever* want to be away from my mum and dad. Now I've been living abroad for years and when my mother asks me when I'm moving back to Australia, I'm not sure what to say.

Alongside seeding these images of my professional life, Dad would remind me that getting good marks would give me the freedom to choose a career like that. And if I saved my pocket money and, later, earnings from my part-time jobs, I would have the freedom to choose my quality of life.

The idea of the 'freedom to choose' became the heart of my motivation and still is today. Even at a young age I was strangely cognisant of this, choosing to study instead of going out, choosing to do fitness conditioning on a daily basis, choosing my high school electives to play to my strengths to get the highest finishing score I could.

'Freedom to choose' also went hand in hand with a strong sense of independence, which in my memory is best demonstrated by the time I announced to my mum and dad, at about eight years old, that I was ready to move out. I was moving into the cubby house. With gentle and intelligent questions ('Where will you go to the bathroom?' 'What about all the spiders?' etc.) they managed to negotiate me out of the idea, but nonetheless, the flame was lit, and there was no turning back.

I was not, however, totally free-spirited. As a child I worried incessantly. I was terrified when I first came to understand the concept of death, and would find myself in a panic lying in my bed thinking about it. This worrying expanded into other areas, of course, and I have vague recollections of child psychologists, flipping dreary monotone meditation cassette tapes over in my white and purple Walkman, and Mum's well-meaning dousing of my pillow in lavender oil each night.

This incessant fear made me shy and, even though I didn't know it yet, depressed. But my shyness was single-handedly eradicated by my year 12 drama teacher, Peter Derrett. An unapologetic, hyper-intelligent disrupter, Mr Derrett taught me lessons and principles I still carry with me today. He didn't soften the world for the classroom. He didn't just walk through the syllabus. He evoked imagination, passion and joie de vivre. He pushed me into a baptism of fire by casting me as Juliet in a school play, and through that tough love taught me:

- You will never be embarrassed or foolish if you truly put everything into what you are doing.

- Always get back up and try again (i.e., reboot).

- The happiest people follow their heart.

Another influential teacher at high school was Mr Quigly, who taught commerce. Commerce just made sense to me. I loved it. But, the subject was only available for a short time, so I didn't revisit this again for many years.

All of this weighed on me in that moment on the kitchen floor. It was my first true experience of a very pivotal moment. The real rite of passage into adulthood—the making of a big decision that only you can make. With few metrics to guide me for such a big decision, I found myself scrambling for reasons to choose one or the other. On the next page is what I wrote down as I looked for pros and cons.

- Dancers were lucky to be able to perform for a living, or even to teach for a living.

- In either of those scenarios, the pay would be low. How could I build the next generation on such a low salary?

- My guess is that, like in many sports, dancers had an early expiry date.

- I wasn't a top-of-the-class amazing dancer.

- I loved dance. My drama teacher, Mr Derrett, taught me 'the happiest people follow their heart'.

- A law degree meant a good base of knowledge that I could leverage in lots of industries.

- I'd spent my time in high school focused on the arts (dance, drama ...) and I knew I didn't properly understand how the world worked. If I took law, while it wouldn't be a natural fit, it would teach me the world in a way that would be to my advantage.

- An international business degree would surely be a step in the right direction to achieve a life that looked like the pictures my dad had painted with me as a little girl.

- And ultimately, if I really didn't like law, surely I could change my career? Go back to dance?

Fiona stared at me, gobsmacked that I would even consider law over dance. She knew me well and in that moment, could probably see more clearly than I could.

I chose law.

Six cups a day

My first year of law and business school was brutal, haunted by a feeling of regret for the path not chosen. I found myself at each semester break on the phone with my old dance teacher, in tears, looking for some guiding light, some comfort that I'd made the right choice. I tried continuing dance training at a local studio, but, without being able to dedicate the same number of hours as I had previously, it was a frustrating exercise in thinking my body could move like it used to, and finding with each step that it could not. Eventually I stopped attending class and stopped my daily dance exercises.

During these days I fell into a weird routine that showed me exactly what happens when you do something that your heart isn't in. I would regularly sleep until 2 pm, then buzz into lectures fuelled with six cups of coffee in a bid to keep my brain switched on to engage with the content. I scraped through exams and assignments with the lowest effort possible, which resulted in the lowest passing marks possible. My essays were an embarrassment, my energy entirely devoted to trying to keep myself moving forward day by day, rather than actually learning. I found it impossible to concentrate on the long passages of legal language and hated myself for my poor marks. It felt like my brain was in molasses.

I wondered how I would ever make it through the full five years. But the idea of dropping out was impossible. To not keep my promise to myself to learn this, not keep my promise to my parents that I had truly made my mind up on my path in life? I had mentally constructed for myself just one viable path to follow, and that was to finish my dual degrees in law and international business.

Painstakingly, I stuck with it. It felt like a cage. But it didn't have to be that way. In hindsight, the best piece of advice I could have given myself would be to look for ways to enjoy it. To get curious about law in a way that really meant something to me, that fit with my passions, values and beliefs. Reflecting on this now, it's possible that I didn't even understand what those beliefs and values were then. Today I am clearer about this, and conscious that these will continue to grow and evolve too.

I am also very aware of how glossy and perfectly impossible that piece of advice to my younger self is — to look for ways to enjoy something I was hating. It's easy to know better more than a decade down the track, with what feels like many lifetimes more experience of the world and myself since then. Interestingly, that lesson is still worth reminding myself of today, on those mornings when I pad around doing tasks that are the least important because I am avoiding the big scary task that I don't know how to do. Yet as soon as I sit down and let myself focus on it, it's absorbing, it's interesting, and it's ultimately very rewarding to crack something entirely new.

During my third year of university, one of the major law firms' local offices had a huge litigation on and my flatmate, Peta, had heard they needed a small army of paralegals to work through the due diligence. Somehow I managed to snag one of the positions. (I put it down to their desperation for able people, not anything to do with my talent, given my middling grades.) This blossomed into a summer clerkship, which turned into a job in the mailroom, which turned into a job offer on graduation.

I felt like a fraud. Had I tricked the system to somehow land this role in a top-tier firm? How long till someone figured me out?

During graduate lawyer orientation and training sessions I was constantly watching my graduate colleagues, wondering if they'd spotted the cracks in my capacity or qualification to be there alongside them. They never mentioned it, but I still wonder if they knew. This sense of fraudulence grew into an accepted self-perception for me. A habit, if you will. And some habits never die.

I found my niche very quickly in banking law. It was one of the few subjects I'd enjoyed at uni (alongside jurisprudence, and in particular a class called 'legal fictions' where we dissected pop culture against jurisprudential theory, but I hadn't found a way to weave that into a career). And the people around me were incredible. It turned out that the years I'd done in the mailroom served me well, having given me a practical application of the processes that surrounded banking. It would take me many more years to understand that I learned by doing.

Within my 2.5 years of banking law I tried insolvency litigation, banking, finance and securitisation. Immersed in interesting work, surrounded by incredible minds, my attention was held but my heart was not. I was demotivated yet again. I wanted to shine at my work but I was failing to engage with the papers in front of me. I started making simple errors and, while none ultimately slipped through the net, that, alongside my mood dropping further and further, showed me something had to give. And so came that inevitable moment.

'I had an awesome day!'

I was at dinner with my friends Matt and Jess Newell. Matt, who worked in advertising, asked me how my day had been. It had been the worst. I was working through an insolvency case that I was finding personally challenging. I gave a short version of the overly long day, and then asked Matt, 'How was yours?'

'I had an awesome day!' he replied.

When he said that, something just clicked. I hated law. I had to get out. To do that, I had to finally face what I'd been avoiding since my first day at law school. I had to make some clear decisions and take action.

In hindsight, this was another important lesson that I can only today articulate succinctly. Sometimes, the momentum of life that we build for ourselves simply becomes our life. We forget to keep making conscious decisions. We forget to keep checking in with the life we want for ourselves, our values, our vision. I had gone to law school not to become a lawyer, but to learn a new way of thinking. To qualify myself for other dreams. But, here I was, a lawyer. Not looking at any path other than becoming a partner or in-house counsel. It had to stop.

While today I can tell you with clarity how I figured myself out, rest assured, at the time it was messy, frustrating, exhausting and emotional. It felt like it might take forever to get an answer—or that the answer might never come. And even when I did come up with an answer, I didn't know for quite some time whether it was the right call or not.

In many ways, even as I write this book, I am in that place again. I'm asking myself really messy questions like 'Was that a fluke?' and 'Have I peaked?' The mind is a brutal companion. We will come back to that later. For now, here are the steps I took.

I came to a realisation that when I chose to study law, I had not known what law was in the day-to-day sense, as an industry: what a good day looked like, what the bugbears were — and what I could and could not live with. And now that I was thinking of changing careers, I didn't want to leap from the frying pan into the fire.

So I began to quiz every person in my life about their career. From close friends to acquaintances at events, I'd eagerly enquire about how their day had been, if that was usual, what kind of tasks they'd done, what success looks like, what the industry was like. The questions went on and on. And as I climbed into that research rabbit hole I realised that I would need to marry up these findings against the things I wanted out of my career. Otherwise, I'd risk choosing something that one of my interviewees loved, not something *I* loved.

My list was an uncensored mix of work and personal life values, applied to career. It was something like this:

- Whatever it is, my life must incorporate creativity.

- I need to be in an industry that is about creating something, not taking it apart.

- To have the opportunity to really be thoughtful in my work rather than simply having it be a means to an end.

- Yet it does have to have an end! It needs to have a good degree of commerciality for me to work with.

- I desperately want to be in an industry that is less rigid in its regulation and processes, and instead more intuitive.

- Ideally, I want to be in fashion or beauty.

- I want to work in a team, to learn from people who are great at what they do.

- To travel with my work.

As I read this list again today, not much has changed.

In the end, advertising was the industry that piqued my interest. It seemed to have most of my list neatly tied in a bundle. And Matt Newell mostly had good days at work, so there had to be something to it.

I researched agencies and met with as many people as I could. But the truth was I'd already fallen in love with an agency I wanted to join: The Campaign Palace. They had a page on their website dedicated to their values. As I read them I felt like I'd found my tribe. The values, the people, the work. Everything I read told me that this was not just a fit for the kind of career I wanted, but would also serve what I believed in too.

One morning, amid all this personal discovery, the partner at my law firm walked in with about 27 folders of due diligence and had them set up in my office. My heart sank, but my stomach felt very grounded. I knew what I had to do. I closed the glass door and cold called The Campaign Palace. The next day I interviewed with Sasha Firth, the head of account management and group account director, and, a few days later, resigned from law to move into advertising (taking a 50 per cent pay cut along the way).

As I spoke to each of the partners to say goodbye, one in particular will always stick in my mind. He said to me, 'Ah you're going to do something creative. Of course. I mean—look at your shoes!' That day I was wearing a pair of cobalt-blue fish-skin kitten heels. I smiled, said thank you and walked out the door.

CHAPTER 2
CHOOSING TO TRY

It was the summer of 2008. In Australia summer means long days stretched out on the sand at the beach, salty hair, the smell of sunscreen, and my favourite—the feeling of a warm breeze around bare shoulders.

At that time I had been working in advertising for just over a year. The Campaign Palace operated in a very flat corporate structure, so in a short time I'd had exposure to all parts of the brand-building process—brand strategy development, media-buying strategy, the creative process and, finally, execution. There was a lighthearted sense of quirky fun that permeated the workplace and a lot of learning on the job that I loved. I was finally starting to understand that I learned best by doing and I started to feel at home.

Michael Fox and I had married in September 2006 and moved to Sydney in 2007. He'd started out with a graduate stint in law at Clayton Utz, another major law firm, followed by a graduate role at Super Cheap Auto. At that time, it was the fastest growing retail business in Australia. Michael was the first graduate they'd taken on, and under the wing of the CEO he was given an in-depth operational experience of the entire business, alongside him doing his MBA. The program shifted significantly after his first year and he went on to Google, at the urging of his best friend and a groomsman at our wedding, Mike Knapp.

Mike had worked at Google from very early on in the establishment of the Australian office. He'd graduated law and IT, and was now working as a software engineer at Google's headquarters in Silicon Valley. (To minimise confusion, I'll only refer to Michael Fox as Michael, and Mike Knapp as Mike.)

Finding our Purple Cow

We had all ended up at Broadbeach on the Gold Coast that summer, a beautiful, long sandy beach on the east coast of Australia.

We were lying on the sand kicking around ideas. Mike and Michael had both recently read Seth Godin's book *The Purple Cow* and had been watching clients at Google achieve stratospheric success thanks to growing consumer confidence in buying online.

The premise of *The Purple Cow* is to develop a concept so interesting that people cannot resist sharing it with others. Imagine driving past a field and seeing a purple cow in it. Now tell me you wouldn't share that on social media.

We kicked around ideas from ugly sweater kits, to — well, to be honest, I don't remember all of the ideas. But we fell upon shoes at some point.

I had recently made a stopover in Hong Kong after learning from Michael's mother, Jenny, about a store there where she had designed her own shoes. I loved the idea and desperately wanted to try it out.

I had dashed from the airport to Hong Kong Island, winding my way through a cramped street market before finally finding myself in a shoe store roughly the size of a small market stall.

The warm lighting and neat beige shelves with gold finishings were a welcome refuge from the multisensory assault from the alleyway in which the store was located. I glanced dubiously at the rows of shoes, none really to my liking. There was absolutely no hint that I could design my own. Was I in the right place?

An older man came out from the back room and I explained I would like to design a pair of shoes. He nodded and bustled to the back room, returning with piles of swatchbooks and a sketch pad.

This man was Mr Tin, who would become our first supplier.

That day I discovered that designing shoes was a lot of fun. The myriad colours, textures and shapes were incredible. I designed 14 pairs in 1.5 hours — surely I'd broken some kind of record. I returned to the airport elated with excitement.

Ten weeks later the shoes arrived in Sydney. As I wore the shoes I got more and more questions from my girlfriends — largely because the shoes were designs they'd never seen. When I explained I'd designed the shoes myself, they asked if I could have shoes made for them too. The excitement about the prospect of designing shoes was unanimous. The reasons they cited — 'I can never find shoes in my size', 'I want to make shoes with a lower heel', 'I can't find the style of shoes I'm looking for' — would later become key parts of our consumer insights.

Sitting on the beach, we reignited a conversation that Michael and I had with his family the night before — designing your own shoes online. We got talking about how excited every single woman was when we told them about the concept of designing their own shoes. How *I* had felt when I found out that I could do this. We talked about the shoes I was having made for my friends, how many pairs I'd bought, how much they cost, how long it took for me to receive them, how I'd designed them. It really felt like it could be a Purple Cow idea.

Lying on the beach, feeling the sand shift under my beach towel as I propped myself up on my elbows talking about starting a company — it didn't feel extraordinary. It was a relaxed time of year, heading into holidays and time with family. My mind wasn't racing as it normally did over endless weeks of work; it was relaxed, imaginative and curious. I didn't feel lightning strike. I didn't have a burst of 'knowing confidence'.

While I knew from my law days about company structures and setting up a business, there was a lot I didn't know about starting a business. I was a good saleswoman (I'm still proud of that time I sold over a thousand dollars of The Body Shop product in one transaction when I was 18), but I didn't have an inside scoop on marketing, PR, financial modelling, fundraising, bootstrapping, conversion rates, manufacturing, making shoes, doing business in China, e-commerce, ROAS, COGS, CAC, LTV, and so on. (Don't worry if you don't know these terms — I'm intentionally doing that so you feel the same discomfort I did at this stage. I'll explain a lot of these later in the book — no need to pull up Google right now!)

And, all that aside, I definitely didn't want to just instantly drop everything.

I did know that I loved designing my own shoes. I loved the idea of everything I'd learned in my career thus far, the skills I'd built and the savings Michael and I had made, providing us with the freedom to explore and potentially choose to start this business. I felt curious enough to explore it a little further.

I admired various businesspeople but I wasn't an avid reader of business biographies and business books. I didn't have a swathe of theories that I was aching to put to use. I just had a curiosity. I know there are many out there who would have had much greater ambitions than I did at that point in the journey, but I didn't. I just looked at the next step, then the one after that and the one after that.

It gave me a sense of comfort that both Michael and Mike had observed this world of entrepreneurship. The fact that they were curious about the idea too validated for me that it was worth exploring. I just felt that there was nothing to lose. And, if this did work out, and we were financially successful—maybe, *just maybe*—I could take myself and the next generation of my family into even greater freedom of choice.

It was an itch I wanted to scratch. But how to begin?

Going from idea to action

In the weeks and months that followed, we researched. Was anyone else doing this? Were they doing it well?

I pulled out my old university books from my degree in international business and started to think through things. What were the Strengths, Weaknesses, Opportunities and Threats of the idea?

How would the business model work? How would we make money? And then Michael and Mike prompted questions from their fields of expertise—for example, how would people use the website to design shoes?

And, on top of all of that, how on earth would we make shoes? How are shoes made?

When I thought about solving all these problems at once, it felt overwhelming and far too difficult to achieve anything. It was like trying to push a whole pile of boxes through a doorway at once: you're bound to get stuck. But if you take them through the doorway one by one, you'll eventually get everything through.

That is, if you can convince yourself to stop procrastinating. This was my enemy number one, and the beginning of a painful relationship with myself in finding the line between inaction and creating the mental space for creativity and recharging. I knew that I needed down time to really percolate my ideas—to help them take form properly. But how would I know when I'd had enough productive downtime and was now just wasting time? It's not that I wasn't excited about the idea; it was that mentally, I was in a hole that I didn't yet know was depression.

Through our research we found that there was really only one company attempting to do what we wanted to do. And even then, the user experience was poor, the materials were not great, and the designs on offer weren't appealing.

Then there was, of course, NIKEiD, now called Nike By You, that allowed customers to adjust the colours and materials on a limited selection of sneakers. We'd heard that the customisation area of their business had grown to around US$100 million in revenue per annum within a short period of time. This felt validating—we took this to mean that there was a market for customising shoes.

Finding your MVP

If we took the success Nike was having with customisation and put it into a women's fashion shoe label, surely that was a formula worth testing. And so we began the journey to understand what we would need to do to build a 'Minimum Viable Product' to test this idea. And, yes, this was the first time I'd ever heard the words 'Minimum Viable Product' or, if you're super hip, 'MVP'. Mike had experience with this process at Google in building software, so I learned about the concept from him, and it seemed to make sense. Put together the most basic version of your idea, show it to people you think are your target audience, get feedback, and then you know what to invest more time in for the next version of your idea.

Or in more theoretical terms: You need to validate your idea through both qualitative and anecdotal research that provides compelling support for the idea, both for you and the team you hope to build. This is incredibly important because, particularly at the start of a business, the hours are long, the work is difficult and the pay is low. So it's important to do everything you can to show that all of this is worth it.

Here are some of the research questions Michael, Mike and I asked ourselves when we were thinking about our idea and MVP:

- Do people want to buy this product or service?

- Are they looking for it on Google?

- Are they asking about it on forums?

- Are they talking about it on social media?

- Are they trying to use existing products and services in a way that would be better served by a tailor-made solution to that problem?

- Who else is doing this?

- Who are the industry players?

- What do I need to learn from the current industry players?

- How big is the industry?

- Which geography do I want to start in, and end up in?

- How much profit does the industry generate in the market in which I want to play, annually?

- How can I take a share of this?

- How would people find out about my product/service?

- What would the most compelling key message be for customers?

- What's better or worse about the way I think this should be done?

- What's my unique selling point?

- How big can this business be?

- How big do I want my business to be? Do I want to build a large global business, or a lifestyle business for me to run?

- Does this business idea scale efficiently?

- What would the business model be?

- How would I receive payment?

- Are there tax issues I should consider?

- How does this fit with the current regulatory framework for the industry?

- What resources do I need to start my idea? (cash, hires, equipment, etc.)

- How do I rally these resources together?

- Do I need to raise cash? Should I do it through a loan? Venture capital? Friends and family?

- Do I need access to experts in this industry?

- What roles would I need to hire?

- Do I know people I can talk to about this? If not, how do I meet them? Are there networking functions for this industry?

- What would be exciting about this idea for the people I want to work on this with me?

- What would a basic 12-month forecast look like for this?

- Can this business break even? And if so, when?

- If I think this business could be sold to someone, who might that someone be?

Our list kept becoming longer and more detailed, which is exactly the kind of thinking and research that should go into the idea at this moment, before making any significant resource investment.

When we finished our research phase, we took a breath and then set about step two, which was pulling together what we'd need to make it happen.

Just remember — if you also decide to create a list of research questions like we did, I would recommend that you give it parameters. There is a point at which you will learn infinitely more by simply doing rather than planning. So define a limit. Maybe it's a time limit, or maybe it's a milestone limit as to what you need in a minimum viable product to start showing people and get feedback. It can be risky to launch when you know the product isn't perfect, but you can also manage expectations — 'We're just starting out and we'd love your feedback'.

Just don't get stuck at this stage. You'll never be fully ready, so jump in and start the business before you're ready.

CHAPTER 3
NAMING OUR IDEA

As the idea progressed, Michael and I found ourselves drawing our friends into naming discussions over brunch, dinner and drinks. The name of our company had to be somewhere and fresh eyes were always helpful.

As we sat together speaking various words out loud, they felt silly, unnatural and awkward. We'd often preface saying the word with 'So I don't think this is it, but ...' and at times we'd just dissolve into laughter saying words to one another. Argh. Nothing just stuck. In this part of the business journey I really was looking for a gut response: a feeling to tell me we'd found the right thing. But as that was absent, I needed to find some tools to help me figure it out.

I started to look at the names of everything—shops, furniture, even bands. It made me laugh to realise that some 'brands' we just take for granted and accept in the day-to-day are actually super weird. For example, I'm sure 'Pearl Jam' or 'Red Hot Chili Peppers' were not instantly natural names for bands either. My point being, until you give the words meaning they are simply that. Words.

Throughout the entire process we kept thinking about brand names that we each loved. We thought about what made them impressive. Usually it was the way the word sounded, how it felt to say the words, and how easily it could be remembered. We repeated 'Google, Zappos, Mimco' out loud—hoping these names we loved would somehow help procure our own brand name.

On the very practical side of things, as we brainstormed we kept our laptops close by to check the availability of the business name and domain name as we worked. We also looked at whether there were other businesses using that name that we might end up competing with to 'own' that word, or that might cause confusion for our customers when they searched for us online.

I then went through three stages of brainstorming. I don't know that there truly are 'three stages' to brainstorming a name—this is simply what organically happened as we felt our way through the process.

Stage 1: Defining the brand insight and territories

I'd spent a lot of time thinking about this. Why did I and the women we had spoken to in order to validate our concept find this idea so exciting? I'm at my best when I visualise, so to help myself unpack this I had covered three pages with scribbles in pencil, felt-tipped pen and texta that only made sense to me. It's funny how these little techniques can really open up our thinking. Some people go for a run; I like to draw.

It seemed to me that women like me were always on the hunt for fashion. Whether I was browsing online, flipping through a magazine or just walking down the street, I would mentally snapshot things I saw that I liked. A skirt, a handbag, a pair of shoes ... Sometimes I would even stop the person and ask where they got it from. (For the record, I still do this. It's partly for me, so I know where to find the item, and it's also for the person because I think it's really flattering to be asked this.) And then I would find myself hunting for it.

Hunting.

The idea formed for me that women hunt fashion: women are 'predators of couture'. This kind of statement feels quite high-end, because of the category (fashion) and that word I'd used to describe it: 'couture'. However, functionally, no other word could work in its place (except perhaps 'shoes'—though even from the beginning I wondered if bringing shoes into the brand name would prevent us from entering other categories). The trick for us was that we weren't going to be a luxury brand, and we didn't want to pretend to be. We wanted to be a creative, reliable, young brand that could help you to realise yourself as a shoe designer and find all the shoes you'd ever hunted.

Okay. So. Predators of couture. Where to next?

I needed to take this seed of an idea and build out a full identity for this brand, which luckily I'd experienced at The Campaign Palace.

Building a brand identity

There are so many elements to work on when building an identity for a business. The most accessible way I found to approach it was to imagine it as a person. This technique is not new — perhaps one of the best ways to unlock this approach is the time-honoured concept of 'brand archetypes'. I'd come across the concept for brand archetypes at The Campaign Palace, shared with me by one of the kindest, smartest men in the game, Mark Sareff. This concept consisted of the 12 types of consumer and described the traits of each. I would strongly recommend taking a deeper dive into this concept if you're in the early stages of building a brand. Here are the 12 types:

- caregiver
- creator
- explorer
- hero/champion
- innocent
- jester
- lover
- magician
- outlaw
- regular girl/guy
- ruler
- sage.

I picked two archetypes to build from for any brand I worked on from scratch. As I read through the descriptions of each, our idea was the creator and the lover. The creator helped people to craft something new, express themselves. The lover built community and was, well — kind of sexy. I saw our brand as helping women create something that made them feel amazing. I specifically wanted to avoid exclusivity or alienation.

The combination of these two archetypes seemed to provide that foundation. This gave us a clear direction on brand personality very early on.

Defining our territory

Now armed with a concept and archetype foundations, I had to take a run at the actual name again. But this time, I decided to choose areas or, as I called them, 'territories', to deep-dive into. No-one really told me to do this; it was just the process I put together.

After a lot of scribbling on A3 pages I came up with a few territories to explore — sort of like themes to focus on at the middle of a mind map.

- an actual name — for example, Jodie; but I really didn't want to use my own name, as it seemed like hubris and I never wanted to risk having to 'give away' my own name if we sold the company or something along those lines
- hunting
- myths/legends of the female huntress or warrior
- words or customs in other languages and cultures that related to the huntress
- wordplay using a shoe-related word mixed with hunting words or concepts.

The process of exploring these territories yielded a lot of names. Honestly, all too weird and silly to even list here.

This exercise also revealed to me that we didn't want our name to be too dark and menacing — something hunting is commonly associated with in pop culture. This was a good discovery moment. And although this helped open up some really rich brainstorming areas, it didn't yield a name.

Stage 2: Guided brainstorming

When we felt we'd explored the territories I'd defined to exhaustion, we looked for new prompts to inspire us. Naming resources and experts are extremely valuable, but in our experience they were too expensive and time-consuming for a barely-started business without any budget. So we looked for free online resources and Micheal came across the Igor Naming Guide. This methodology suggests thinking about naming by:

- *Doing a competitive analysis.* If many competitors have followed a particular path, you can differentiate easily.

- *Not trying to describe your business in your name.* Brands always appear in a context that describes the business. Let your brand name do something productive.

- *Remembering that names built upon Greek and Latin roots can be seen as cold.* Examples given in the guide are Acquient, Alliant.

- *Thinking of poetic, rhythmic names.* They're great as people like to say them and they seem warm and friendly, for example, Google, Zappos, Kleenex, Oreo.

- *Trying to come up with evocative names.* These are bigger than the good or service. They evoke the positioning of the product, rather than the good or service, for example, Virgin, Apple, Yahoo — however what they evoke must match the brand.

- *Remembering that taglines are important.* They can help brands rise above their product or service, for example, Nike — Just Do It, Apple — Think Different.

This process gave us endless lists of possible names ...

- *Muckluck:* A soft leather boot. While the word itself just felt really rhythmic and poetic to say, in addition to being shoe related, it risked giving consumers the impression we only sold that specific style of boot. And the sound sort of felt a bit casual; more casual than we wanted to position ourselves.

- *Veruca Salt:* The character from Willy Wonka who knows exactly what she wants but cannot have, in other words, just the type of woman who would want to design her own shoes. But, probably not great that verruca is a type of wart that appears on the sole of your foot.

- *Scarpe:* The Italian word for shoes, and also sort of poetic and fun to say.

However, again, this didn't yield a name. Nothing really seemed to be 'the one'. I was starting to wonder if perhaps we should simply pick one, and go with it. Maybe I'd romanticised how I'd feel about the name.

Stage 3: A bottle of wine

My friend Lisa Lovick, a colleague and fast friend from The Campaign Palace, and I were sitting in the small courtyard attached to my one bedroom apartment in Surry Hills. We'd picked up some sushi from our favourite local place and I'd cracked open a bottle of wine. Her cat, Gremlin (honestly, she was so cute and definitely looked like a gremlin), wove around our feet as I talked over all the names we'd thought of but ultimately had passed on. Lisa was throwing a name to me and I'd say one back. We would sit silently for a moment, let the name sink in, then keep going.

After a while we were sitting in chairs facing one another, knee to knee, in some kind of trance-like state, just saying name after name after name. Finally Lisa, with her hands on her temples, blurted out 'Shoes of Prey!' Suddenly all those romantic notions I had about how I'd feel once we had the right name were there.

Filled with the kind of energy that comes from the joy of a breakthrough, but wanting to check that we had it right, I then ran it through a series of practical tests.

Firstly, we wanted to make sure that this worked for people who weren't as close to the subject matter as we were. So we went out to test it. Which means my patient friends, colleagues and acquaintances were (again) poked and prodded with my questions on how they felt about this business name. We found that women connected with the name, understood the insight immediately and appreciated the duality of the word 'Prey'. Men, however, didn't understand the name unless the insight was framed up prior to being told what the brand name was. They generally liked the name, but felt it didn't make sense.

As owners of this name, we also had other concerns—what if we branched out from shoes in the future? How would we use the name then? Should we not attempt to develop a name that is not so connected to a single product? We decided that this wasn't going to be a deal-breaker. If we did expand our product offering, we'd deal with it then.

We were happy to discover it was available as a URL. Which meant that we would totally own the traffic attached to the name.

Forging ahead

To be completely sure, we brainstormed again, using Shoes of Prey as our benchmark. However, a new name never came. We collectively decided that the fact that men didn't connect with this as women did was not a great concern, because we were only marketing to women. Once the brand gained momentum and popularity among women (fingers crossed!), men would be accepting of the name on this basis, and by the way women behaved in relation to the brand.

I made an attempt at creating a logo, scribbling a woeful page of concept drawings. Cate Stuart-Robinson, another Campaign Palace colleague, looked it over and asked why I didn't just sign the words and run a needle underneath them. Duh. I did, and we were ready to register the trademark.

The application process was pretty simple, until we found that the word 'Prey' had already been registered in our trade category.

Urgh. We were gutted.

We went back to the drawing board, but still nothing stuck. We very nearly went back to Veruca Salt, but the trademark issues were much more challenging with it, it really *couldn't* do the job that Shoes of Prey did, and, honestly, *verruca is the name of a wart on your foot.* No. Nope. Nuh-uh.

Maybe we could find another way. We contacted the owners of the trademark, offering to buy it. They turned us down. They thought they might have a use for it in the future, even though they hadn't used it to date.

I felt so frustrated. Like when you see someone else has your name as their handle on social media, and yet has never made a post.

We ended up venting about the topic in our blog posts. (We'd created a blog as a way to share our journey with friends, family and colleagues. It also helped to have people outside of the business share thoughts on how we could tackle tricky issues.)

We also vented over brunch and, aside from being a bit monotonous for our very patient friends, it was helpful, because a lot of people in our social circle were ex-lawyers. One in particular pointed out over poached eggs and avocado that this particular trademark was about to hit a 'use it or lose it' deadline. Which is exactly what it sounds like: if you register a trademark you have to put it to use in a certain time frame, or you lose the trademark.

We contacted the trademark owners again and told them they could either sell it to us now, or we'd file for them to lose it. They replied saying that they would sell it to us, but only if we included a pair of shoes for their respective girlfriends.

It was a done deal.

Finally, we were Shoes of Prey.

Phase 2
On Building and Determination

With so much theory in place about how this could work and a few key foundational items in place, it was time to really find out how this would work. And *if* it would work. We needed to go and talk to the shoe makers.

CHAPTER 4
FINDING SUPPLIERS IN HONG KONG

Michael and I had just attended the wedding of our friends Alex and Cynthia Rous in Bali, Indonesia. It was our first trip to Bali (confusing, I know, given that we're Australian and should have been there many times over by the time we were 27 years old). Since we were in the region, we'd decided to fly from Bali to Hong Kong to visit Mr Tin's store and others we'd found out about in our research.

We didn't know if these stores were fronts for factories, or if they were simply retail brands that had suppliers who made their shoes for them. We didn't know exactly what the outcome of this visit would be. However, it seemed like the right lead to follow, so we went to learn what we could.

We decided that we needed to scout out all the stores to understand their aesthetic and the quality of their product. We'd do this dressed in our casual clothes so that we'd look like and be treated as consumers. We only wanted to spend our time in longer conversations with the stores that had product of the standards we wanted. In Hong Kong at that time English was very prevalent, so communication was not an issue.

Of the stores we visited, we found two or three we really liked. The next day Michael and I went back to these stores in our business attire, armed with business cards and our idea. Somewhat to our surprise, the initial pitch and approach did get us in the door.

Just like Teenage Mutant Ninja Turtles

I looked across the table at Jennifer, our potential supplier. She owned a store in Hong Kong and a factory in China, along with her family. She was a 30-something woman with dark, straight hair, and, although both her figure and stature were slight, her energy was not. She was a force from day one. She seemed to be constantly analysing us, letting moments of silence linger a second too long, making me feel as though she was adding us up as we spoke. Outside, the steep, narrow streets of Hong Kong were shiny with rain. Sitting in front of her on the table was my flimsy business card with a small clip-art bird motif in the corner.

She was asking about our order quantity for each SKU. I explained (again), 'It would be one pair. The customer will build their shoe design using our software, and then we will make that one pair of shoes for them, and send it to them, wherever they are in the world'. She sat back in her chair and explained, somewhat perplexed, that usual minimum order quantities were much higher. While she was technically able to make one at a time, she simply didn't see the business in it and encouraged us away from it. She looked down at her small spiral-bound notebook, expressionless. I couldn't shake the feeling that she thought we were totally, completely insane.

I could see her point; their entire business model was optimised for large orders. Taking time out to commission a mould for the heel shape you like, source the material you described, and so on, is not the scalable part of their business. It's the gateway to their real business, which is large, consistent orders.

We knew it would be challenging finding someone willing to make us a sample without a large order, and it would probably be expensive. And the way they developed that sample might not be easily transferred over to another factory, should we decide to go elsewhere. We hoped to get around these issues by showing our projections based on marketing and sales plans we had built. Of course, none of this was guaranteed, but we had to start somewhere.

What experience did I have making shoes? None.

What experience did I have in starting a business? None.

But here I was, with my clip-art business card and a vague idea about how it would work. I was asking the questions I needed answers to. In every single way we were kicking off this idea well before I was ready.

Yet as it turned out, it was the perfect time to do this. The Global Financial Crisis had begun and large factory orders had slowed down. They had capacity to work with us without a lot of risk. And ultimately, Jennifer became our second supplier, after Mr Tin, the man I had first designed my own shoes with.

The stores we met with that day were all attached to factories in China that were making their unique shoe designs, on demand. We had found exactly what we were looking for.

Today when I reflect on those first meetings with suppliers, I think about all the other people with an idea, who have been the crazy person in the room. I invariably start chuckling to myself thinking about a cartoon I loved as a kid, *Teenage Mutant Ninja Turtles*. Imagine the first pitch for this idea. 'Ok guys, it's going to be awesome. There'll be four brothers, named after famous classical Italian artists. They're the size of human adults, but they're TURTLES, and their teacher is a RAT! They're all ninjas who fight crime and, get this, their enemy is *a brain in a jar.*'

Crazy.

Insane.

Amazing.

An enterprise that today carries an unreported but no doubt large value given that its movies alone are said to have grossed over half a billion dollars.

But not everyone could have made such a bizarre idea such a huge success. In the same way that not everyone could build a business like ours.

Our meetings were almost always multiple hours long, with varying degrees of language barriers between us. Largely they were on our side, as neither Michael nor I spoke Cantonese or Mandarin. Invariably English was spoken on the supplier side, which I personally always found impressive. I also felt embarrassed that I had so few Cantonese or Mandarin words in my vocabulary. I tried to learn on a number of occasions, each time mastering a little more, but never reaching anything approaching fluency.

Cultural differences reared their head early on, when one of our suppliers invited us for dinner. The restaurant was a large open room, well lit and full of round tables of various sizes. The far wall was lined with tanks filled with the fresh catch that would become dinner, as is common in restaurants like these. I don't recall exactly how the ordering happened, but I do remember finding a large, rubbery, orange goose foot on my plate. I'd read about the importance of not shying from strange foods at business dinners in China, so I watched my supplier casually take bites from one across the table as we conversed. I mustered up my courage and took a bite. I couldn't ignore the texture, the flavour, the idea of what it was as I chewed, but I kept up my poker face. Then, for the rest of the meal I proceeded to try to keep up very engaging conversation with good eye contact, not only because it's polite, but also to distract from the fact that I'd hidden the remainder of the goose foot under a lettuce leaf on my plate.

Although in principle we made our agreement to work with our first and second suppliers early on, it would take several more meetings for us to figure out *how* we would work together. Mike spent weeks in Hong Kong with our suppliers, building our relationships while also analysing shoe silhouettes, textures and angles as he built the first version of what the elements of the shoes would look like as you designed online.

And even after all of our meetings, nothing was written down other than the emails we exchanged. We had to prove ourselves to be a worthwhile partner over time. While I normally wouldn't have approached a business relationship this way, the fact was that we didn't yet know what the relationship would be. We both had to learn if there would even be a relationship worth documenting.

Sourcing your own suppliers

Not all supplier sourcing needs to be this time and resource intensive. Depending on what you're looking to make, there are a few different ways to find suppliers that are right for you.

If your product already exists

If you want to make a product that already exists, I'd suggest searching online for your suppliers—it could be as simple as finding them on Alibaba or LinkedIn.

If you need to learn about the industry

If you aren't totally sure of exactly the product/service you need or if you need to do a number of products, it's a good idea to go to a fair that relates to your field. In Hong Kong, for example, they hold the Canton Fair every year. It runs over a pretty reasonable period of time and within that, the weeks are broken up into industry themes. Manufacturers exhibit samples of what they can produce, so it's a good way to see what can be made to help you make a decision and to have some initial discussions with the manufacturer.

If you want to do something totally out of the box

If you want to do something totally out of the box like we did, something that isn't already being made or needs a totally new process to be made, then you've got a much more high-touch journey ahead. You'll need to figure out who makes the product you're after and then talk to them about what it is you need. This method requires a lot of time on the ground.

Another idea ...

One final option is to find suppliers who supply brands that are in a similar area to you. This is often a bit more difficult to find out than you might think—while the factory may be happy to tell you, the brand often treats their supplier as a secret source.

CHAPTER 5
MY FIRST CHINA TRIP

Once we had established some relationships, we asked our Hong Kong suppliers for invitations to cross the border into China as their guest (which was necessary to get a China visa as Australians). We needed to visit to:

- understand how each component of each shoe went together, and which of these were interchangeable; for example, could the stiletto heel on that strappy shoe also go on this boot?

- decide what combinations of options we wanted to provide to our customers

- see the shoe factories we would work with from an ethical point of view; the more we understood about how the shoes were made, the better we could seamlessly integrate our systems and processes into theirs

- source all the other products that we would need to be able to ship shoes: shoeboxes, shoe dust bags, tissue paper, letterhead, heel pads, toe pads and envelopes.

Mike, Michael and I reached the first factory and were ushered into a boardroom. I was dressed in what I thought of as my sourcing uniform: I would hide my jewellery and wear something really simple. Black trousers and a black silk tee. An unbranded oversized handbag and simple shoes. I knew that negotiations on price were intense, so I wanted to go in looking presentable: serious, but not splashy.

Fluorescent lights shone down on the oversize table. Prototype shoes, heel moulds and scraps of leather were stored on a few shelves in the corner. The cupboards were all a dark chipboard laminate. There was a small bar fridge in the corner. People filed in to take a seat around the table and the meeting began. After initial pleasantries, a review of where we had progressed to on our business and how it would connect to our working relationship, we asked to see the factory floor.

We walked into a large warehouse space lined with rows of machinery. There were high ceilings and tables with low overhead lighting to give the hundreds of cobblers good light to see the detail of the shoe they were working on. Standing workstations stood among shelving at the top of the rows, with computers tracking stock, progress and more. We watched as every single person seemed to be totally occupied among the cacophony of sound rising from the floor. The smell of leathers, glues, new materials … it was like nothing I had experienced before.

I began to wander into one of the aisles and was quickly pulled back. It wasn't till much later on that I would learn that I'd been ushered back so quickly because the owners were concerned that I might learn some of the secrets of their factory, whatever they may be. Perhaps I would talk to the staff, learn the number of staff and stations to work out about capacity and quality. Perhaps I would learn they were making shoes for someone who wanted their supply chain to be confidential.

I'd say we had reasonable success in these meetings, however there was always a friction point for the supplier in discerning whether we were tyre kickers or a viable business that they would want to supply.

One of the reasons factories charge significantly for first-time samples (or will simply turn down doing them at all) is that it's only worth their investment of time and resources (even if you're willing to pay them well for it) if large, consistent orders will follow.

Slowly I began to realise that the suppliers I was meeting were wearing great jewellery, and driving nice cars. They were showing me that they had a successful business. I realised that I needed to wear my jewellery, dress well and pull out that brand-name handbag. It signalled from the instant we met that I had a viable business with money to spend with them, rather than being a tyre kicker who was not worth the trouble of meeting with.

It was obvious to us that we needed local help to navigate this part of our business.

Our first hires in China

As we continued to eke out our supply chain while preparing for pre-launch, Mike and Michael were spitting their time between China and Australia, working on technical and operational aspects of the business while I continued in my day job, working on Shoes of Prey in my spare time.

We quickly realised we'd need full-time help on the ground in China. We knew that our supply chain would be complex and critical to our success, and we were also painfully aware of the industry, language and cultural skills we lacked. This was the obvious skill gap we'd need to fill.

We found Alice, our first employee in China, through our personal networks. She joined us for a three-month stint, and helped us to find connections through her networks and employment agencies. Largely, building hiring networks was a successful strategy; the only time this created problems later down the track was when we didn't do enough due diligence to realise we had at one stage hired a large portion of one family, which created a lot of avoidable people management challenges when they attempted to flex their family muscle in our business. But hopefully if you find yourself in the same position, you'll now know to check and prevent these same issues.

Alice helped us find Vanessa Iron, our first permanent employee in China. Vanessa spoke quickly, excitedly—almost nervously—but truly lived up to her surname when it came to negotiation. Her nature was sweet and her work ethic was second to none. Vanessa set up our first 'office' in China very early in the piece. We needed somewhere to base ourselves, store packaging and samples, and to pack and ship the shoes from.

Vanessa brought on Qun, a quiet, slender girl who would become our longest standing employee. One of my greatest pleasures on the people side of the business was sharing the journey with Qun, watching her go from a girl in her early twenties to meeting her husband and becoming a mother. Each time I walked into the factory after some time away, she would touch my waist and my wrists and, turning to someone to translate, tell me with a little smile whether I had gained or lost weight since I'd last seen her. I held my breath every time for her verdict.

Vanessa and Qun were responsible for daily interactions with our suppliers: logging shoe orders, ensuring they were on time, quality assuring shoes when they were received, dealing with packaging suppliers, testing delivery services providing tracking updates on shoes, dealing with local banking for the company and more. They were complex, vast operational roles. Being on the ground regularly in China, sharing our wins and collaborating with Vanessa and Qun on building out our systems and processes built the foundations of our supply chain in China.

Don't drink the soybean smoothie

It came time for me to spend my first really meaningful amount of time in China. Michael and I scheduled a five-week trip to Guangzhou, about an hour over the border from Hong Kong by train.

It was our third week into the trip and we were in one of the many small villages in industrial Guangzhou, where our office was located. This was a hyper local area, with Michael and I the only Caucasians around. In our hotel room, a thick, roughly woven bed base pressed through the inch-thin mattress, poking my body no matter which way I turned. The tropical humidity hung in the industrial city, the stifling, thick heat only just kept at bay by the stuttering air conditioner standing in the corner of the room.

My stomach churned, lurched and cramped yet again and I tucked my legs to my chest to try and ease the pain. How had I gotten so sick? Had I accidentally swallowed tap water in the shower? Was it the food from MFC (the local take on KFC)? Or was it the soybean smoothie I picked up from the street stall? WHY DID I GO TO THE STREET STALL??

Through the fever of nausea I glared at the wallpaper—a slightly too murky shade of pink printed with far too much ink, making it look like the pattern was dripping down the walls.

In these first weeks as I'd walked the village to find my way between the hotel and the office I was completely disoriented. I'd travelled outside my comfort zone before, but nothing could compare to this. I couldn't read anything around me. I couldn't communicate meaningfully on my own. The day before I'd ended up in a 20-minute miming session with the hotel reception just asking for more pillows.

The television in the room blared incomprehensible ads for skin whitening cream, watches and whisky. The only points of familiarity that I'd encountered in three weeks were a can of premade Nescafé coffee with milk and a bottle of Dettol that I'd managed to buy to wipe the room down when Michael and I first arrived. (Trust me on the Dettol.) Somehow, in the thick of industrial China, I'd heard rumour there was a Papa John's pizza store a 30-minute car ride away (surely they delivered) and a Starbucks (where English was spoken) a 45-minute car ride away. Neither of which I'd had time to go to.

We spent long days in our first China office, which Vanessa had found and rented for us. It was a small, tiled room with two folding tables, three plastic stools, fluorescent overhead lights and shoes. So many shoes.

Despite the discomfort I was curious and loved having the opportunity to be a participant in these towns. One beautiful distraction was a little boy and his family who lived across the road from our office building. On one of the first days, I'd noticed this tiny little boy, surely only a few weeks old yet already with soft straight hair gently floating above his face with perfect rosy cheeks, in his mum's arms. It was a little slice of familiar domestic bliss that stood apart from the hectic, overwhelming experience of the first days in Guangzhou.

From the office I would go to local markets to source materials, decorations, heel shapes, packaging and more with Vanessa. The sourcing markets were a series of tiny stores — perhaps 1.5 metres wide and 3 to 4 metres deep. They were all within a large building of five to six floors and because of the setup there was no natural light inside. To top it all off, the closed, overfilled spaces were often in a fog of tobacco smoke.

Snakeskins hung on the walls in folds from the floor to the ceiling (a sight that still scares me) and large expanses of soft leather were laid out in piles as high as my waist. Brightly pigmented suede sat in rolls on shelves. Once you pushed past the sensory invasion and focused on the materials, the market was an absolute treasure chest.

My first few visits were overwhelming — I'd come back with bags and bags of samples, millions of ideas and feeling seriously concerned that I would never be able to whittle down the items we'd actually offer to our customers as options to use in their shoe designs. It was a debate that ended up lasting many years into the business. Our customers designed the product, and at this stage we believed that our brand and aesthetic needed to somehow be open to all ideas that our customers wanted to bring to life. It needed to include all ages, all styles, and not force people to follow a prescribed style as so many labels did.

But of course we had to have some limits. The trick was to have a range that felt limitless, but also that felt simple enough to make a decision from. This balance between choice and paralysis from too much choice for our customers would be a constant struggle.

Those early days were so long. At the end of one long day of sourcing by myself (I'd ventured out alone, having perfected my hand signals and a few key Mandarin words), I left the leather market to find fat drops of warm, industrial-town rain were falling heavily. The crowd was plastered against the building under the awning. I saw a free taxi heading in my direction and stepped out into the downpour (my samples were all wrapped in plastic, safe from the rain). As the rain hit my skin I felt a huge sense of relief—these warm drops were the most comforting thing I had felt since being there, and in that moment I felt acceptance. The environment was tough, but also beautiful in its own way—and I wanted to be part of it.

As our visits went on I felt a sense of life, time and its significance by watching the little boy across the road from our office grow. The little peanut in his mama's arms became a bigger boy mastering the ability to grasp objects and cry out for his mother's attention. He and his family will never know the connection between their journey and that of a stranger in the building across the street.

And as for that one horrific night of food poisoning ... well, I haven't had a soybean smoothie since.

Assessing factories quickly

As we built out our supply chain, we became adept at quickly assessing factories. We'd wanted to continue to look at other shoe factories to reduce our risk of being beholden to one factory, and to learn about how other factories made shoes. Observations and a few key exercises would quickly provide indicators as to whether this was a factory we'd want to work with.

We wanted to make sure our goods were really being made in the factory we were working with. (We had heard that factories would almost always say yes to an order, and if they didn't have the capacity to complete it, the order would be outsourced to another supplier.) We also wanted to ensure that they were compliant with our ethical and environmental standards.

Aside from receiving assurances from them, we'd do our own investigation by paying unannounced visits to our suppliers.

We wouldn't even give our driver the address we were going to. Maybe we were being paranoid, but if we did give the address, it gave the driver the opportunity to call ahead to the supplier to warn them we were on our way in exchange for a payoff.

When we arrived we would go straight to the factory floor to check ethical standards. I'm really glad to say I personally never once saw a breach in the factories we worked with. Then, we would ask to see specific orders that were at various stages of completion. If they weren't there, we would be able to deduce that the item had been outsourced to another, unapproved factory.

We did find this to be the case on one occasion. The quality of our shoes had changed dramatically, and the supplier had unilaterally extended the delivery times. Discovering that they had actually sent our shoes to another factory that we had not approved allowed us to take control of the situation and return to the prior quality and timing levels by insisting that our orders be made in house, or a much lower price be given.

We always wanted to be sure we were dealing with the person who ran the factory, the decision maker, especially if we were visiting a factory we'd not worked with before. China tends to be hierarchical, so generally speaking it's fair to say that the boss has the biggest, nicest office in the factory. So, we'd ask our contact to show us their office. Sometimes this was enough to catch them off guard and it would become clear that they didn't have an office. If they did take us into their office, we'd linger and start some conversation in the office to see if they tried to move us on quickly. Their behaviour in that room generally told us if they really were the boss. If we found that they weren't the boss but we liked the look of the factory, we would do what we could to meet with the actual boss. If not, then we would wrap up the meeting quickly.

We wanted to know if the factory was doing well, and if they had kept their exclusivity agreements, so on the unannounced visits we'd take a look at the number of people on the factory floor, and whether they were idle or busy. We'd also sneak a peek at the names on the boxes being shipped and at the brands on their production lines.

One of the best books I read on this topic was *Poorly Made in China* by Paul Midler. I'd definitely recommend reading it before you do a trip to China if you're planning on working with factories there.

Our supply chain was taking shape, but would it work out in the world? How would it be received?

CHAPTER 6
TESTING, TESTING

We were so much further along than I ever imagined we would be. The mechanics of how the shoes would be made seemed operational. It was time to step up in the 'Maslow's hierarchy'-like needs that a company must have to survive. Did the experience work in practice? Did people like the experience we'd built? How much should it cost?

Beta testing

As the first version of our software was completed and our first suppliers were engaged, we not only spoke to as many women in our lives as we could about our idea, but we also asked them to be our first customers.

I sat in meeting rooms at Google Sydney at lunchtime, delivering shoes and receiving feedback from colleagues of Michael and Mike who had participated in the beta test. I did the same with women at The Campaign Palace and with friends we'd invited to try it out as well. We gave them our cost price for shoes they designed on our early software in exchange for candid feedback. The feedback was varied, interesting and very candid. 'If you stuff up you should just own it,' said one tester whose shoes arrived after the estimated delivery time. Blunt and fair. The greatest friction I had with this was that we simply could not address it all. I felt confused about what to focus on, and just wanted to please everyone. Between Michael, Mike and me we broke the list down and prioritised it, but in those first days of hearing the feedback, it was difficult to organise it into something actionable.

We then got a stall at the local fashion market on Sundays at Bondi Beach. We never sold a huge amount, but the discussions we had, and the feedback we heard, told us endless amounts about what worked and didn't work about our idea. The other benefit of being at these particular markets was that they were frequented by fashion editors. Many years later they told us that they had seen us at an early stage of the brand. It built an element of shared history in our brand, which I loved.

During this time we were working out some kinks in the ordering process. One of the most difficult was the issue of how to get an accurate shoe size from our customers.

Red herrings

Our first supplier had suggested to us that we simply ask people for their shoe size when determining the size of their shoe. We were reticent to do this; we felt there had to be a more accurate way. We were custom-making shoes, after all. So during our beta testing phase, we went on a long search for the solution to finding the right size the first time you bought our product. Today this concept is the entire premise of some retail technology companies that have started since our early days of fumbling with size and fit.

Avoiding at all costs the simple solution of just asking the customer to tell us their shoe size, we went down a few different rabbit holes.

We tried making a YouTube video with detailed steps on how to measure your foot with a piece of paper, pencil and ruler. If you didn't have a ruler, we'd have one online that you could print out. Before we even tested this we learned that the margin for error was large. Printing out a ruler meant having to make a series of checks to ensure that the printer didn't change the scale of the document. As for taking measurements, we had thought this would be done by putting the foot on paper and marking specific points. But we were soon to learn that about 20 per cent of women have feet of a size that don't fit on an A4 page. And the difference between shoe sizes is six millimetres, so using a thick texta or making the markings at an angle could throw the size out easily. Not to mention the hazard of having raised the customers' expectations to imagine they would be receiving perfectly fitting shoes after going through this elaborate process.

Still, we had our beta testers (who were still found from pools of our personal contacts — old colleagues, friends, family) measure their own feet following our instructions. Then we measured their feet using the same method. The results were abysmal: only 16 per cent were consistent, and every beta tester reported back that the process was slow (it took about 20 minutes) and tedious.

We also tried measuring the lasts (a last is the foot-shaped piece of material that the shoe is built around and is pictured below) and supplying the measurements to the customers. They would then tell us what size last they wanted. But it turned out to be misleading because if you selected the last that perfectly fit your foot, that would have your toes pushing right up against the inside edges of the shoes—very uncomfortable.

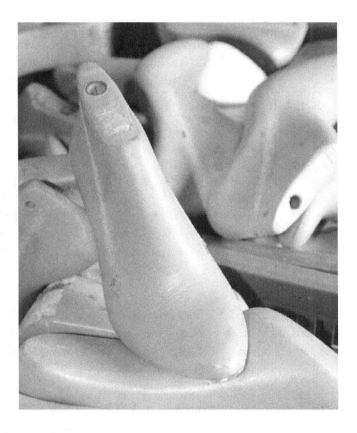

We also considered creating a database of brands and shoe sizes. For example, if you tell us you're a size 9 in Jimmy Choos, we could match that in our database and make you an equivalent size. We loved this idea, but soon realised that task would be like starting another business. And in fact, years later another company did start that business.

We looked at existing measurement apps on smartphones, but none of them were capable of giving us the suite of dimensions we needed for the foot. We even considered whether there was a way to send the customer something that could take a mould of their whole foot. As you can see, we were really in the weeds. Much too deep into the weeds of a problem that wasn't core to the service we wanted to offer as Shoes of Prey.

The sizing conundrum was one of the catalysts for opening that market stall at Bondi Beach markets: we could set up sample shoes for people to determine their size. Unfortunately, that was totally unscalable at these early, bootstrapping stages.

In the end, after significant time and resources spent on testing, we ended up back at the beginning: just asking for people to tell us their shoe size. It gave us 80 per cent accuracy the first time around.

Sometimes, the simplest solution really is the best.

Setting the price

As we approached the launch of the business, we had to set our price. We looked at a number of items. But firstly and most importantly, we set out to understand the breakdown of how much it was actually costing us to make shoes and get them into the hands of our customers, while providing them with the level of quality and support they deserved. Otherwise known as ... Cost Of Goods Sold (COGS). It includes everything involved in making the product.

So let me be straight up: I did not know what COGS were. I had to learn it. And I learned it through Michael, who was focused on this area of the business. In our business COGS were a bit of a moving target. You'll see why.

COGS for us were basically materials, labour and shipping. This remained a challenge throughout the entire business, as no two pairs of shoes were ever the same. Every shoe used a unique combination of materials, components and time, so to do any reporting at all, we needed to start off by working with averages.

Like any fashion brand, we continually added new materials and styles, which in turn continually expanded this matrix.

On top of COGS, we also needed to factor in a percentage for returns, given that we had decided to have a generous returns policy for our shoe-lovers. (They could return shoes to us within 365 days, unworn, and we would refund or remake their shoes.) The way we thought about this was to consider industry return rates and then adjust over time as we had more and more data to understand what our return rate would be. For the shoe industry in general it was 33 per cent at the time, but our return rate at Shoes of Prey would turn out to be much lower. We then distributed that cost evenly across the number of sales we expected to make.

I realise that in the customer's mind it may feel jarring to read that returns are built into the price you pay. If you didn't return your shoes, why should your price cover someone else's decision to return theirs? But conversely, what if you had to pay a large fee to return a product? My personal guess is that it would be an affront for customers and not a good look for a company.

We also had to factor in overheads such as rent, electricity, coffee and tea for the office—the general stuff that adds up! Then there are the costs that are not directly connected to the making of the product, but that are still incurred to sell the shoes: marketing, non-revenue generating roles in the business, and so on.

We also took into account factors such as currency value and fluctuations, on top of taxes required to be paid for the countries to which we shipped.

Then, margin is on top of this. It varies by industry. At the time, apparel retail was 200 per cent. (For comparison, beauty was 400 per cent.) For example, if it cost $100 to make a dress (materials plus overheads and marketing, etc.), the retail price of the dress would be $300.

We ultimately used margins that were smaller than the industry rates. There were two reasons:

1. We weren't planning to sell our product wholesale, so we didn't need to put a margin on the product for ourselves and the end retailer. We would be the end retailer.

2. Our production costs were very high, but we anticipated being able to reduce these over time with higher volumes and relationship improvements.

Then we looked at the price point we came out at to see if it fit with the brand we were building. We thought through:

- where the price positioned us against competitors
- how our quality compared to the market
- whether we were high end or mass market (or both!)
- whether we were aiming for mass market or a niche
- our target audience — age, salary, disposable income, and so on.

We ultimately landed on A$250 as our average price point.

But how to apply it across so many styles with so many varying COGS? We would have to pay our supplier per shoe, so our COGS would be different for every single shoe. And building out technology that could dynamically price the shoes as you were designing them was going to take a huge amount of resources and might be confusing to customers. What if you designed your dream shoe and in the end, it was way out of your price range?

In the end, we decided to start with only four different price points depending on the general style of shoe being designed. For example, all ballet flats would be one price, simple heels another price, stilettos and boots another price. Not the perfect solution, but it allowed us to start the business without having to build out dynamic pricing technology.

Our first website

With all our technology coming together and the supply chain looking solid, it was time to design our first website. It was built in Flash (a multimedia and software platform that can be used for animation) and had a black background with hand-drawn outlines of shoes that interchanged with one another, and some seriously amateur product photography.

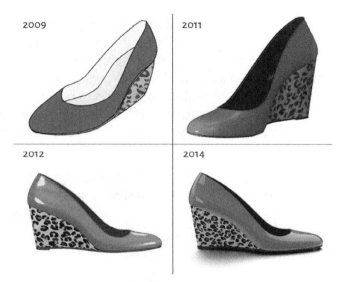

2009 2011

2012 2014

The progression of our shoe design images over time.

We couldn't afford a photographer for our product photography and figured it shouldn't be too difficult to take a photo of a pair of shoes on a white background. Michael and I pulled some white sheets out of the linen cupboard and draped them over kitchen chairs to form a horizonless background. We didn't even iron them. We were just seeing how things worked, and, well—they didn't. I still laugh today when I look back at these first photos.

The first shoe photo. Yikes.

Michael found someone who had taken some photography courses who introduced Michael to the idea of a light box. This was a white box with one side left open, where you put the lights and camera. The shoes sit inside the box. This would control the lighting conditions, removing reflections and shadows. He bought some foam core board from the local art store, we ordered some cheap lights online and decided to try again. This time, we enlisted our friend Cynthia to assist us and the images took a step in the right direction.

I fussed with the shoes to figure out what angles made sense, and, although some of our first images had some pretty incredible ratio issues, at least they were clear and we had *something* to show our customers what the end product might look like.

We sold millions of dollars of shoes using these images and our dark website built in Flash. Our images improved slowly over time, but of course we could have made this journey shorter if we'd had the funds to simply hire a professional photographer.

Luckily, our friends Cynthia Rous and Andy Miller were photographers, Cynthia much earlier in her study of photography than Andy, who had a really beautiful eye. We worked together on the first brand images for the website. Brand images were pictures showing the shoes being worn in context to help create a sense of lifestyle. Perhaps of feet tucked up under a coffee table. Perhaps while walking on a footpath in the city. Perhaps in a boardroom, owning a meeting. Because the idea of Shoes of Prey was that women liked to hunt couture, I decided that the imagery should be angled downwards, and show legs in movement with the focus crisply on the shoes. I wanted the imagery to mimic the moment when you see a woman walking past wearing great shoes and you take a mental snapshot of them to go and look for later.

These images were much more successful than our first founder portraits, which make us look like a set of awkward siblings, and my headshot, which makes me look like a grumpy designer. That wasn't any reflection on Andy's skill; we just had no idea what to do in front of a camera.

On original founder portraits.

Source: Andy Miller.

Needless to say, we came a long way from this!

Photography starter guide

If you're in the same position we were, here's a very quick starter guide.

Camera: You can take photos on your phone if a camera isn't in your budget now. And there are great apps, such as VSCO, to help with that. (I think I just set up this book to be outdated fast!) There will always be newer apps and technology to help you take better photos, so do a little research before you start.

Zoom: If you're using a camera, avoid using a wide-angle lens as this will distort your product. If you're using a zoom lens, don't zoom all the way out.

Hold steady: Next you're going to need a tripod or something to keep your camera steady, as this affects the sharpness of your

(continued)

Photography starter guide (*cont'd*)

photo. If you've got customers zooming in, that's important. Slight movement causes the photo to be blurry, and that's not great for product photography.

Light: Once you're ready to start, consider your light. I'd say lighting is one of the most important things. If you don't have lighting, find a room filled with natural light. Natural lighting is wonderful for photos. Find a place with even lighting to avoid shadows.

Soft light: You also want to consider aiming for soft light as opposed to hard lighting. Hard lighting happens when your light source is smaller than the object and soft lighting happens when your light source is bigger—this is what you're after. So find large windows and avoid flashes unless you're using a diffuser to soften that flash. (You can also use a plastic bag as a diffuser.)

Infinite white space: If you're trying to create a white background, one of the most popular ways to do that is by creating an 'infinity curve': basically a white wall with no horizon or edges. You can do this cheaply by using a white roll of paper or board and curving it so there's no edge. Of course, the bigger your product, the bigger your roll will have to be. If you do this, you want to light in such a way that no shadows appear behind the product. It should look like it's in an infinite space.

Colour balance: Before taking your photos, make sure you set your colour balance properly so that the colours in real life look like the colours on your screen. You can edit things afterwards, and you will, but it's always best to get your colour balance correct in the process rather than trying to fix it later.

Angles: These also affect the way your customer interprets things like scale and design. Once you find the angles that work, be consistent with them.

Styling: If you move away from white backgrounds, or if white isn't an appropriate background for your product photo, styling becomes much more important. There are lots of great tips on the internet for this depending on your product and how to fill your scene, so I'd say think about what you're after, what you're trying to achieve, and research how others recommend you achieve this.

Repeat: Definitely take more photos than you think you need! You might think you've nailed it in one shot but there's no harm in taking a few, especially once you start touching up photos and seeing more detail on your computer. Sometimes when I download shots onto my computer I realise things like that they weren't totally in focus, which means I can't use them.

Post: You will be editing your photos once they're taken, and I'd say it's safe to say that filters are not a great way to go about product photography. Editing photos is a whole other beast and there are a lot of great tutorials out there on how to edit photographs, but it's definitely a large part of product photography.

Good luck—I'm sure your pictures will turn out a lot better than our first ones did!

Phase 3
On Launching and Commitment

We could have spent so much longer tinkering with Shoes of Prey. There were endless lists of things to do. There were endless things I was unhappy with on the site. And I did campaign against Mike and Michael — I just wanted a little bit longer. But, they were right. More polishing wouldn't matter. Either the idea would stick and we'd need to invest more time in it, or it wouldn't and we would save both our time and energy to look at something else.

CHAPTER 7
READY?

My parents were pottering around me. I was glued to my laptop: the final details of the deal were coming together. My mum and dad are avid gardeners and, although I was only living in a rental, they assured me the garden would be worth it: it was easy work, and they were having a relaxing time landscaping the courtyard, which had been neglected by years of renters and a somewhat cost-conscious, nonchalant landlord. I stopped for a minute to percolate a thought, poured my dad a cold beer and took it to him. As he looked over their progress he said, 'You know, no-one has done this because they couldn't see the start.'

It amazes me how parents have this ability to drop an absolute gem of insight over a mundane moment on a Wednesday afternoon.

I would revisit this moment many times in the years to come, when I was stressed and in the thick of things: If I could just see the start, I could move forward.

All in all, it took us nine months to go from tossing around ideas on the beach to launching. In some ways that's quite quick — but it could have been even quicker. We definitely got snagged on things we need not have. When you have spent time passionately dreaming out every detail of the business or project you want to launch, it can be tricky to decide which parts of it you will need to forgo at launch — because if you choose to launch only when everything is perfect, you are likely to either:

- never launch
- invest too much in things that you end up scrapping because they don't work in practice.

You may recall an excellent example of this: our sizing debacle in chapter 6.

Sometimes I get asked when I 'knew' that this idea could work. I didn't ever *know* what would work. I didn't bet on success. I loved the idea of a world where you could design your own shoes, and the potential that could apply to multiple categories. But that's all. I was curious and I had two smart co-founders who were equally curious about seeing where this would go. It wasn't until much later, when we had established a steady flow of sales, a strong Net Promoter Score and funding from accomplished, intelligent investors that I really believed we would have the chance to go so much further.

A totally unceremonious launch

In late August 2009 Michael was working on Shoes of Prey full time and, while I was still at The Campaign Palace, I'd accrued a lot of holiday leave. So we decided to fly to Sicily to spend time with my family during the summer.

I had spent time with family in Italy since I was a little girl, and I treasured everything about being there. I loved the smell of the air: a fragrant mixture of the ocean, espresso, oranges, pastry, tobacco, and gasoline from the Vespas that buzzed past. I loved the buildings, perfectly aged with artfully deteriorated sconces, faded yellow and salmon-pink facades, and forest-green and dark-brown shuttered windows. I loved the playful, theatrical humour of the people and the sound of Italian being spoken. As a child I was fascinated with the patterns in the mosaics, on walls and on ceramics. I felt both at home and inspired every time I set foot in the country.

It was the first time I had taken a partner with me to Sicily. (I wouldn't have dared take anyone with me until I had a ring on my finger; there was still a very conservative bent to the older Sicilian generations. It just wasn't worth causing gossip that would reflect badly on my nonna and cause her stress.)

Michael and I started our days with a jog up the beach to the bottom of the cliffs, a swim afterwards (unless the tide had brought all the jellyfish in) and then back to the old house we were staying in — snacking, chatting and, of course, working on Shoes of Prey.

By early October 2009 everything we'd been working on was 'ready'. We had a website with working software. We could accept transactions. We could make shoes. It wasn't perfect, but it was ready enough to sell shoes and learn what we could do better from shoe-lovers who didn't know us personally. Mike was eager to make the site live, to see how it would fare in the real world. I felt uncomfortable. I wanted more imagery. I wanted better copy. I wanted ...

I was scared it just wasn't good enough. I urged the boys not to launch it, and they urged me to see that we should. And they were right, so we did. When it launched I was in Rome with my friend Steph, and I watched the site come online from the hostel we were staying at. I felt a huge mix of emotions. It was so exciting, a little scary, and also didn't feel completely real.

There was nothing particularly ceremonious about the launch. It just set into motion an entirely new set of priorities. This time, everything we did could affect customers or potential customers.

Our first sale was perhaps the least scalable experience we could have had. In the first 24 hours of launch we were all a bit unsure if we'd launched something people wanted. Michael was responsible for customer service and had 20 emails back and forth with a customer, answering her questions. Finally, she purchased a pair of shoes. Our first genuine customer who didn't know us personally.

We knew we needed to get the word out to drive traffic and sales. At this stage we didn't have a marketing budget, so we looked for ways to get the word out ourselves. Our first project was to send our friends and newly gained email newsletter subscribers a link that would give anyone who clicked on it a $50 credit towards their first purchase. Both the email and the credit link could be forwarded. We put tracking into the links in the email and found that it alone drove over 10 000 visits. On average, the email had been sent on four or five times. And it translated into sales. By day five we had sold four pairs of shoes in one day and we could see there was potential for this to be a business that people really did want.

Deciding whether the side hustle should be the main hustle

Michael, Mike and I were sitting in a macrobiotic sushi restaurant in Surry Hills on a Sunday. The chef was known for her overzealous attention to detail. She wouldn't even keep staff — she didn't like the way they cut carrots, she didn't like the way they served customers. She only liked her way. The wait for food was always a little long, but it was great food.

Maybe it wasn't coincidence that we were sitting in an under-resourced restaurant with a great product when we hit on the conversation about when to add our next full-time resource ... me.

So far we'd funded the company with our combined savings, and bootstrapped our way through these first few months. None of us were drawing a salary, and we had a lot on the line with so much of our savings invested.

Mike had been the first to start working on Shoes of Prey full time, to build the site. Michael and I had split our day job salaries with him to share in the risk. Next Michael had gone full time, to build out the operations, and we split my little advertising salary between the three of us. Now it was time to build out marketing, communication and product.

I felt excited and scared. Finally, I would focus on Shoes of Prey full time. But it was also terrifying. What if it didn't work out?

Having a business 'work out' can mean different things to different people. It could be:

- the earning potential — remember my focus on freedom to choose from chapter 1
- being profitable
- securing funding
- opening a store
- making your parents feel proud about what you're doing.

The list is endless, because it's personal.

My idea of having a business work out was a combination of earning the same salary I was on in my main hustle, and making my parents feel proud.

Making my parents feel proud had a lot to do with being financially independent. To put that into 'real' terms, I mean being able to afford to own a home, to eat healthily and provide any future generation with the same or better education opportunities as I'd had. While I knew that my parents would be proud of me in many scenarios, I knew that this was the most important one to them. And more than that — I felt they were right.

Michael and I had been married for almost three years, we had a house deposit saved and I was progressing quickly in the advertising agency. Was it worth risking this financial independence on this very big 'what if'?

When I truly looked at my fears, the questions swirling in my head largely boiled down to four main concerns:

1. Will I lose my foothold in my current career trajectory?
2. Am I capable of doing this?
3. What if I lose everything?
4. Would I still be lovable if I failed?

As I talked these concerns out with my co-founders, who had both already gone through this process, we found the following, very compelling counter to each question.

Will I lose my foothold in my current career trajectory?

I have this weird (read: human) tendency to really blow things out of proportion, so I tried to reposition my perspective to remember that if I were to fail at this, it would not be the last thing I did. There are no dead ends, just journeys that give us experience. If we even had the smallest amount of success in starting and running a business, the experience I would gain should push me forward, not backwards in terms of my career path. It would teach me how to think like a leader, be really immersed in resource management, learn how to run finances and much more. All of these skills are important to career progression in the vast majority of careers I was interested in, so it could only be a good thing.

Am I capable of doing this?

Now this was a big one, because it's a question only I could answer. And you might have picked up by now that I am not my biggest supporter. (Remember my impostor syndrome throughout my career in law.) So I stripped it back to the facts. (I find looking at facts the best way to stop my mind from sabotaging me.) Here's what I came up with: I'd got great marks at school. I'd completed a law degree. I'd worked for a top tier law firm right out of university, and successfully switched careers into the exact advertising agency I'd wanted to be in.

Yes, I am capable.

What if I lose everything?

I had to think about what losing everything meant, because it's a multifaceted concept. Of course it meant money, but it also meant pride, reputation and a whole host of other things that were much less measurable but no less painful than losing money.

At this point we started to talk about that often bantered phrase 'fail fast' and it really clicked. If we do fail, it's better to fail fast than slow. If you're going to try something, you should action it quickly and effectively and understand if it will succeed or fail so you know where to put your energies in the next part of the journey.

If we just played around the edges of this concept for weeks, months or even years, only to find out that it didn't work, then it would be akin to a slow and painful death. And it might make you wonder: maybe if you'd gone all in, it would have worked out.

As it turns out, I'm not one for what ifs.

Would I still be lovable if I failed?

I have a really close relationship with my family and friends. They're the people I can go home to when I make a bad decision or something doesn't work out, and they'll tell me that I'm usually smart, and that tomorrow will be better.

I knew that if I failed, I wouldn't be a different person. I would still live by my values — I would still know who I was, and so would my friends and family to whom I could look for the priceless things in life, like love and support.

I had also looked at other hugely successful businesses that had experienced failures. If we did fail, we wouldn't be the first. I'd heard that the Dr Seuss books, the most popular children's books in the world, were taken to 76 publishers before one said yes. That's a lot of 'failures' before succeeding. I'm not saying you should doggedly run every single idea to the ground before giving up, but I am saying that fear of failure needs to be pushed to the side rather than allowed to dictate the outcome.

So I went into The Campaign Palace the next day and tendered my resignation. Sort of. They offered some vacant office space to us and I ended up agreeing to stay on in a freelance capacity a day or two a week. The office space was an enormously welcome change to our lounge room, and it made us seem much more successful than we were at that point — the large glass windows looked directly over Sydney Harbour. The freelancing, however, lasted for all of two weeks during which I started to understand something about myself that I wouldn't fully connect with until much later on: while some people are highly capable of switching mentally between large projects, I am not. The freelancing quickly ate all of my time, affording me a higher hourly rate but no more headspace or actual hours for Shoes of Prey than I had when I was working full time. So I resigned properly this time. Fortunately The Campaign Palace were kind enough to let us keep using the office space.

Finally, we were off and running.

CHAPTER 8
NEW NORMALS

Time started to warp in the most unbelievable ways when I finally worked full time on the business. Days melded into nights, and weekends didn't mean anything other than my friends inviting me for brunch. I'd wake up and pull my laptop into bed to start working, and fall asleep with my laptop on my chest.

My new relationship with time and money

One of those mornings I'd pulled my laptop into bed, I sat in a white Bonds men's singlet and undies, my hair in a messy bun (and I don't mean the chic type of messy bun). I was totally engaged with what I was doing — so much so that I'd forgotten to eat breakfast, move from bed or notice that two hours had passed by. All of a sudden I heard the distinctive Skype ringtone — it was an incoming video call that I had completely forgotten about. I answered on audio and started the call. We didn't really need video for this call; surely we'd just get into the discussion. I thought I'd gotten away with it until the other side said, 'Jodie — we can't see you'.

'Oh, really? Let me check …,' I said, frantically pretending to press keys on my keyboard to 'fix' it. 'How about now?'

'No, still can't see you.'

Flustered, I tried to deflect it: 'Ah, look, I'm not sure what's happening. Let's just continue without it.'

Luckily they dropped it and we moved on with the meeting.

From that day onward, I added an alarm to my calendar invites to warn me about meetings ten minutes in advance.

Time felt sort of ... liquid. I had so much to do and was so regularly in a flow state that I just couldn't keep track of it. Although I wanted to get more and more done each day, I didn't feel like time was passing quickly. I would look back a month and feel like I had somehow crammed a year into it.

Keeping a record

During this hectic time I started to use my diary as my to-do list. It gave me great visibility into what I did every day, and it was one of the best ideas I've come across in a while. It:

- removed that horrible end-of-day feeling of having worked really hard, but feeling like you couldn't name a single thing you did

- gave me total clarity on whether I was prioritising my time correctly. I could see the tasks I was doing, the order I was actioning them in, and what I was bumping them back or forward for.

This exercise was critical in making me a reliable colleague — I was awful when we first started out. I would say 'yes I'll do that' to everything, yet fail to document what I'd committed to or make time for it. And it also became a sort of an exercise in gratitude. Even today, I still do these exercises and I feel myself living about four years' worth of a full life every year. I love it.

From a financial perspective, things were tight. I didn't order drinks with dinner if we went out. I made coffee at home and I ate Maggi two-minute noodles at meal times. (Chicken is the best flavour, in my opinion, and, although I get called weird for doing it, I love putting a whole lot of cheese on top. Not all that nutritious in hindsight, but it was fast, I liked the taste and it kept my stomach full.) I stopped buying new clothing, and when I did they were fast fashion brands on sale. It was a time of pressure for Michael and I, particularly because we were both in the same position.

It wasn't that one of us could support the other financially; we were both strapped to the same fate.

Amid this haze I started to build my personal profile — basically, sharing who I am and why I started Shoes of Prey with Mike and Michael. We'd decided that building my personal profile was going to be an element of Shoes of Prey; we felt it would allow people to understand the brand more quickly, simply for the fact that people register a person more easily than a brand. Of course, there are many scenarios in which it's a good idea to build your personal brand outside of running a business. I'd go as far as to say it's helpful in the progression of most careers.

When we started out I'd had no intention of doing this. I felt that even considering it was somewhat arrogant. This didn't change until one day, when journalist Valerie Khoo invited me for a coffee. I respect Valerie enormously and was flattered that she had invited me to chat. And she said something to me that I will always be grateful for. She asked me why she was only hearing from Michael, when we were a women's shoe label. (Initially Michael had been doing all of our publicity and spokesperson duties.) It didn't make sense. She wanted to hear me speak — she wanted to know my view on the brand. She told me flat out that I needed to start being the person giving the speeches and talking to press. And not only did she tell me this, she then invited me to give my first speech at a City of Sydney event. I was absolutely terrible, but more opportunities to give speeches came up and I took them. With practice I started to get a sense of how to tell our story. I got completely comfortable with my speech content. I started to get comfortable with an audience. And I started to get really good at it.

I began to take the lead on our media engagement. And I had so much fun. I had always enjoyed meeting people, and as I met with journalists it honestly felt more like making a friend (who asked a lot of questions) rather than anything more. Often photos were needed to go along with a story, and so we began to do regular photo shoots and filming for this content, and for our own content on the website and social media. The brand overall felt so much more real when there was a person in it who had a story — a reason for being there.

Public speaking tips

As I got more experienced with public speaking, I learned a few tricks that always seemed to work:

- *Open with a story.* The audience becomes immediately engaged when you start this way.

- *Do everything you can to eliminate fears.* When I first started, I used to write out my speech word for word, print it out and take it up with me. I never needed it (okay — maybe once!) but it gave me confidence that if I truly messed up and couldn't remember what I needed to say, I could simply look down, read, and be on track.

- *If you experience a tech failure, acknowledge it calmly and keep going.* I had a very funny version of this happen when I was lecturing at a fashion school in New York. I almost always check my slides after I've handed them over, but this time I didn't. The computer they were using didn't recognise the fonts I'd used and completely threw out random text throughout the presentation. Which I didn't find out until I started to present. On an early slide I'd put the sentence 'design your own shoes'. But with the font issues, the 's' for 'shoes' had dropped off the slide, and it now read 'design your own hoes'. I said that this wasn't exactly our business model, apologised for the technical issues, the room laughed and we continued on. Hot tip — from this presentation onwards, I screenshotted all my text and inserted it as an image so there were no font issues again!

- *Remember no-one in the room wants you to fail.* They are all turning up wanting to hear what you have to say.

- *Be nice.* As I did more public speaking and had more engagement with press and stakeholders I also learned another important lesson. Being nice, as it was my natural tendency to be, not only made me feel happy, but also got me a long way.

A faltering supply chain

Every Chinese New Year, suppliers close for two weeks to observe the holiday. This normally falls around February or March each year. We'd launched the business in October 2009. In our first year of trade this really crept up on us fast. And I am ashamed to say, it crept up fast and felt overwhelming because:

- we'd failed to be culturally aware of this holiday

- we'd assumed that, just as some people in businesses in Australia work over holiday periods, there would be a similar skeleton staff situation at our suppliers.

In a mass-production business, orders could be neatly arranged around the two-week holiday to ensure that stock was always on hand. The end customers wouldn't even be aware of the pause in manufacturing.

But because our business was on demand and at your door within a promised number of weeks from the date you placed your order, this posed significant issues — particularly when applied to time-sensitive orders such as wedding shoes or shoes for a particular event.

We entered into conversations with our suppliers just weeks before the holiday, sharing our concerns and posing the question of keeping some staff on over the holiday. It's fair to say that our proposal was contentious. Not only did we lack the cultural understanding of the importance of this holiday, but we also lacked a practical understanding of what was required to keep production moving with a skeleton staff. The factory would require sufficient inventory of components and leather to make our shoes over a time during which the component and leather markets were closed. Security staff would need to stay on. The factory normally supplied meals through an in-house canteen. How would the skeleton staff staying on access food if the canteen was closed and most shops in the area were closed too?

Ultimately we worked through these issues with the supplier and agreed to pay much higher rates of salary to those who stayed on over that time to make shoes with us. However, this still didn't work completely to solve the problem because we discovered that there are huge staff attrition rates after the Chinese New Year.

At Chinese New Year, everyone who has gone to the industrial cities for work floods back to their hometown to spend time with family. They use that time to decide whether they will go back to their factory job or not. Perhaps they have earned enough to come home now; perhaps there are other motivating factors. Whatever they are, their impact is significant. Attrition rates, on average, stood at a whopping 25 per cent in most factories. (I'm proud to say that in later years, when we built our own factory, retention rates were very high, and this kind of attrition was nonexistent.)

This meant that after the two-week holiday period, capacity was inevitably reduced for a much longer period while the factories recruited and trained new staff and caught up on delayed orders.

As we started out, our delivery times were around eight to ten weeks. But the holiday caused even further delays, which we had to manage with our customers. Although there were not yet that many, we cared deeply about the experience every single one had with us.

In later years we were far more prepared and adjusted our delivery time at Chinese New Year. We slowed down our marketing efforts leading into this period and we worked with the factory to organise workflow each side of the holiday. But this was one of those lessons we had to learn the hard way.

As we dug deeper into the manufacturing issues, the thought of building a factory that operated on-demand rose to the surface. But right now it felt like a far-away pipe dream. We needed to make a lot more sales before then and we really didn't have a marketing budget to speak of.

Hiring at headquarters

There was never any question in our collective founder mind about the way we wanted to treat our customers. From the brand concept up, we were inclusive, honest, loved celebrating one another and truly wanted the best outcome for everyone. When that came to the coalface of customer service, we decided 'customer service' really didn't cut it, and called our team 'Customer Happiness' and created the title 'Customer Happiness Wonderperson'.

'We're hiring: Extraordinary Customer Service and Startup Wonderperson' was the title of our ad for our first headquarters hire. And the applications came in. We were happily stunned at the quality of the candidates and reviewed them as we weighed up the skill sets on the table.

Eventually, on making the hire, I am embarrassed to say that her first task was, in fact, to figure out how to legally hire herself into the company. Welcome to the early days of a startup.

This person would also work across many administrative items in the company. On reflection, in the early stages of the company, we were really looking for generalists. People who could:

- stretch across disciplines
- not be precious about picking up tasks that were outside their normal mandate or otherwise necessary yet mundane
- spot things that needed to be done and just do them without asking.

Our hire was a highly overqualified candidate who was coming back into the workforce, looking for a flexible schedule. As co-founders we loved flexible schedules too. We had flexibility in spades, and the arrangement worked well — until it didn't. As we started to make more hires and the office was becoming, well, an office, we needed more regular working hours to foster not only the culture but also on-the-spot problem solving as new issues arose. It meant we as co-founders needed to be in the office during office hours, and we wanted our team to do the same. I'm not proud of this but we ended up parting ways perhaps sooner than we should have with this employee, and my management of the situation was lacklustre to say the least.

It felt like we'd failed a hurdle on some of our early foundational values. And I took people issues hard. Over the course of the business, this never really changed. I couldn't quite figure out how we'd gone from genuinely believing and delivering on flexibility to not being able to do either. It seemed insane in a world where the technology for remote communication was constantly improving and we'd purposefully set up our systems and processes to be accessible anywhere at any time. In the crisp, clear view of hindsight, I think we were just at a phase of the company where we did need to be in the same room. We needed contact hours to sit with each other and navigate problems we'd never seen before.

Ultimately, we couldn't afford to sit in the grey area between two approaches or principles, 'we're flexible ... but be in the office!' In this moment we had to think deeply (and quickly!) about what sort of culture is important and accept that we couldn't be all things to all people.

Is customer service a marketing or operational function?

As the Customer Happiness team grew, we realised that strategically we needed to decide — would we think of customer service as a marketing tool, or as a cost of doing business? I've already given it away, I know. But just to confirm, we did of course think of it mostly as a marketing tool.

Each Customer Happiness Wonderperson was empowered with a budget: a range within which they could offer credits, discounts and refunds in situations that didn't specifically sit within our protocol so that after training they could have the power to be able to resolve the customer issue according to their own best judgement.

Secondly, we asked our team to be personable — to always give their name, to always reply having read and understood all the issues in the whole email, reviewed the previous correspondence, reviewed their account. We found out from a friend, Ian Lyons, that, particularly on social media, just signing off with our own real names brought home the reality that there was a human behind the words, a human who cared and was accountable for the correspondence and action items for you as a customer.

We then added phone support. While it was leagues less efficient, it was incredibly important. We offered a customised product; it followed suit that the service should be personal too.

Over the years we dabbled with online chat. I still remember when we had this activated during a YouTube campaign we ran that accidentally targeted a very young (i.e. 13- to 14-year-old) audience (more on that in chapter 9). We quickly shut down our chat function for the week, as the young teens flooded it with chats that quite literally had nothing to do with shoes.

We found that through the combination of these approaches, we built incredible rapport with our customers. They would share fun moments with us, show outfits they had designed shoes for, reply to other customers' questions before we even saw them, and even defend us when an abusive or undeserved comment arose. We would not only go on to perfect and expand on these approaches, but also to figure out how and if they applied to other cultures.

Customer service is cultural

Soon we expanded into other markets. Our first was Japan in May 2010, followed by Russia in September 2010 and then the Netherlands in April 2011. As we expanded our business internationally, we learned that customer service expectations varied significantly between markets.

We launched in Japan in partnership with Yusuke, a serial entrepreneur who contacted us after reading an early article about our business on the Springwise website. Through Yusuke, we learned that customers in Japan had vastly higher expectations than our Australian market. Packaging needed to arrive in pristine condition, and had to be much more elaborate, to communicate the brand and value to the consumer. There were also specific ways to fold wrapping paper and tissue paper that were important to understand. (In Japan there is a ritual of specifically folded material connected with funerals and we needed to be careful not to mimic this in the folds we made in our packaging.)

In order to ensure that the packaging arrived in pristine condition we shipped the Japan shoe orders to Yusuke in Tokyo. He would then put them into the customer packaging, then have them couriered out. The couriers we used were absolutely incredible. They wore white gloves and literally ran the parcels to our customers' hands. (As part of their onboarding to become couriers with that company, there were timed runs up Mount Fuji and orienteering-style exercises to be completed. It was truly phenomenal.) We also learned that it was customary for gift certificates to be re-gifted multiple times before they were used, and so we needed to ensure that gift cards were made from material that would still look untouched after being opened by many people, and find a way to word the gift card so that it did not identify any particular recipient.

These experiences set in our minds the importance of working with local partners when launching in a new country.

While customer service might be an early and obvious place to develop our marketing efforts, we would need to go far beyond this to grow the large business we'd set out to be.

Chapter 9
Telling the World

As I mentioned in chapter 2, the entire idea of Shoes of Prey had been born of the test, 'Is this a purple cow?' Would people be so excited about this idea that they would want to tell other people about it? And when it came to marketing, we (ultimately) approached it with the same test.

The early days of influencer marketing

In March 2010 Shoes of Prey was all of six months old, and 200 000 people had visited the website (which wasn't too bad for a new website.) We were in the early, bootstrapped stage of the business and looking for a funnel of people who would be interested in what we were doing, outside of the traditional avenues. Read: for free.

As we brainstormed, Mike stumbled across the then 16-year-old US-based makeup video blogger Blair Fowler (known online as Juicystar07). She had more than half a million subscribers to her channel and, although her videos were inordinately long (normally around nine to ten minutes each, when the average recommended YouTube video length is just over two minutes), her videos would amass huge watch numbers that were above her subscriber numbers. This audience was very engaged, female and, it just so happened, she had just started doing fashion videos that were doing well. This was a very new and not yet common practice.

This seemed to tick all the boxes.

So he sent her an email that her Hollywood agent replied to. She said that Blair would only do positive reviews, so we should gift her the experience of designing her shoes, and if she liked it, we could go from there.

It turned out she LOVED it. And so, for a small amount of money that I am contractually obliged not to disclose, Blair made a video reviewing our shoes and ran a competition with us for her viewers. The competition required the entrant to design a pair of shoes with Shoes of Prey and submit a note (and the link) in the comments of the video about where they would be worn.

My advertising background made me sceptical about the competition structure. I recalled all the times I'd personally wanted to enter a competition only to find that the entry requirement was to 'describe in 25 words or less ... '. I rarely entered. And, having seen some of these campaigns run, I knew that competitions that required effort to enter meant that the number of entrants was frequently very low. I was worried that the amount of effort we were asking of people would result in not many entries. But the agent was firm and we moved ahead.

How (happily) wrong I was. I had completely misjudged the fervour of her followers and the willingness of the online community to participate. The day Blair's video went live we had 200 000 visits to the website; the same number of visits we'd had in the previous six months.

We were ecstatic. This traffic was unbelievable. But as we clicked through the statistics in real time, the sales chart really didn't come close to the traffic numbers we were seeing. In fact, the sales chart had barely moved at all.

Traffic continued to grow at a huge rate, and by the end of the week we'd had over 530 000 visits to the site. And the competition had more than 90 000 entrants—highly engaged people who seemed to love what we were doing.

The video was the fifth most viewed on YouTube worldwide the day it went live, and it was the most commented-on video worldwide for the day. It was the second most commented video worldwide in the week it went live.

So what was going on? We had traffic. We had really high engagement. Where were the sales?

As it turns out, our rudimentary formula for successful e-commerce of traffic sales was wrong. The audience watching a 16-year-old give makeup tips on YouTube are mostly 13- to 17-year-old girls. And most girls this age, while they legitimately do love shoes and fashion, simply don't have around A$250 to spend on a pair of shoes.

We went into overdrive trying to figure out what to do with this momentum to refine and target it at our audience, now that we'd realised a little more about who that was.

Firstly, we gave the girls the tools to keep doing what they did best — share. We made some changes to our website to make it easier for them to share the shoes they'd designed through the social networks they were using the most to talk about us: Facebook and Twitter. We then ran searches on Twitter to find every conversation happening about our brand, and we joined those conversations and engaged with the people who were talking about us.

And, we took a huge risk. We wrote a blog post about the experience. We disclosed the statistics, the nuts and bolts of what we'd just achieved, and sent it to the business press hoping it would end up in front of the women we thought were our target market — professionals, and women with disposable income.

We tweeted a link to the blog post from our personal Twitter accounts. It was picked up and retweeted by a number of prominent people, including Robert Scoble and Google's AppEngine account. Nearly 100 people retweeted the story and the link to the blog post, and nearly 300 people clicked those links and visited our blog. We began seeing press and, when we woke up the next morning, there was an email from *The Wall Street Journal*—they wanted to write a feature article about it.

We believe this article finally got us space in front of our target audience, because we saw a permanent 300 per cent uplift in sales.

Looking back on the experience, we learned so much on the fly by watching live data. And, because we were a small team we were able to be incredibly agile, executing changes in real time to optimise our initially very poorly targeted campaign.

Handling aggressive online commentary

When you court public opinion online as we had on YouTube, it's never going to be unanimously positive or even neutral. We faced this issue in its full manifestation for the first time in October 2010. An animal rights activist had voiced her concerns about us using animal products (such as leather and snakeskin) on our Facebook page. (For the record, we dropped snakeskin at a later date and introduced fully vegan shoe options.)

I just clicked on this link thinking—'awesome, shoes I can design to suit my wedding dress'. BOY WAS I WRONG, I had no idea it was still acceptable in this day and age to use REAL Snakeskin—that is just unbelievably cruel and disgusting!

Also.... Fishscales??? WHAT THE HELL?

In this day and age when there are extremely nice faux products why do we need to continue to kill innocent animals just for their skin? Why do people feel so very different about how they feel about their family pet, as opposed to a wild animal?

also, for the price your shoes are still generic in style and colour.

In short you are not a true design service—and you stock material that is cruel and unnecessary.

We were so shocked by the message that initially we weren't really sure what to do. Should we take the message down? Did other people think the same thing? Should we reply to her? If we were in a physical store, would we throw her out or have a chat about it?

We weighed up the pros and cons and eventually decided that we had said we were a transparent company. We had said that we would answer people's questions. It seemed disingenuous to us to pick and choose between the questions we answered and didn't. So, while the message tone was not great, the questions she was raising weren't discriminatory, profane or particularly offensive. Had they been any of these, we would have removed the post and put up a note to our community explaining why. In this case, while it was not nice to hear, the questions were fair.

So we left it up and replied to her.

> Hi, thanks for sharing your thoughts and we completely respect your opinion. We've asked previously that the skins are ethically sourced and been assured they are.
>
> We've posted previously about the fact that we're working on vegan materials. Sourcing high-quality vegan materials is possible, but it's actually quite difficult. Finding high quality man made materials that breathe naturally is not a simple task, but we're getting there. We're hoping to be able to launch a vegan range of options early in the new year to give customers the choice of which materials they'd like to use in their shoes.
>
> You obviously feel passionate about this issue and I hope our comments help somewhat. If you'd like to continue the discussion please feel free to email hunter@shoesofprey.com or call us (02 8006 1506). Thanks for sharing your thoughts.

In later analysis, from this we learned that it's good to leave messages like this up because:

- this level of transparency shows that you're honest and have nothing to hide
- this honesty builds trust
- it further demonstrates who you are and what you believe in.

And to:

- reply immediately
- directly address the issue
- provide them with contact details to continue the discussion.

Off the back of this success, we were hungry to keep up the momentum and look for our next big marketing move. And this time, it was the traditional holy grail of television.

Testing television

We were excited to test television. It seemed like the perfect way to demonstrate how Shoes of Prey worked and explain the features and benefits to a large audience. And we got the opportunity to test this theory in our first year of trade. In August 2010, I received an email from a reporter at *A Current Affair*. This show airs in prime time on one of Australia's three large free-to-air commercial stations. It generally has about 1.3 million viewers, which is excellent when considered in the context of the Australian population, which at that time was about 22 million.

I had some reservations when we were contacted—*A Current Affair* is famous for investigative journalism and, although I truly felt we had nothing to hide, I still felt somewhat cautious. This was allayed when I learned that the reporter had a challenging foot size, and had found us in her hunt for shoes.

We prepared for the filming, which was going to be followed by our first magazine cover being shot that same week.

We organised Customer Happiness shifts so that we'd have extra staff from the moment the story aired through till midnight, and prepared our servers to ramp up to handle traffic.

Everything was going smoothly until I said yes to going out for a sail on Sydney Harbour with some friends three days before I was being interviewed. I'd not spent much time on boats and didn't have a good sense of how things worked. At one point, through a combination of bad luck and ignorance, a rope came loose and flicked across my face.

I bent over in pain, holding my face in my hands. My friends yelled at me to look up and show them what had happened—did I need to go to the hospital? Had the rope cut my eye? Terrified about what they would tell me, I sat up and took my hands away from my face. They told me I had a light open graze on my face, from the corner of my mouth up my cheek—nothing too serious.

I waited till we got back to shore to look at my face in a mirror. I looked like the Joker. It wasn't terrible, but it still wasn't great. I called Christina, the makeup artist I had hired to do my makeup on the day (I had no idea what I needed to do to look good on camera) and asked her what to do. She assured me that covering it wouldn't be an issue. 'And,' she added, 'you can just insist that the other side of your face is your camera side.'

On the day of the interview, I entered the room that we had booked out at the office and sat down. The camera crew came in and the room was made surprisingly dark, with a warm spotlight shining directly onto my face. Yep. This felt like it could be an interrogation under very flattering lights. Conscious that I wanted to be natural and relaxed, but also hit my talking points, I sat quietly and waited for a cue to speak. And it turned out it was just like a conversation—with a bright light in your face and a few awkward stops and repeats when we needed to capture something again.

As we waited for the story to air, we set up in my lounge room, laptops on and ready to snap into Customer Happiness mode. The story went live and it was everything we could have hoped for. It focused on the fit of our shoes—we were one of the few brands to offer the size range that we did, along with pairs that had one shoe bigger than the other and other options. We had about 70 000 unique visits from the program—interestingly, much less than from our YouTube campaign. But in this case, the sales we made were immediate and sizable, delivering a number of record sales days and permanently doubling our sales in the Australian market.

This started to tell us a lot more about who our customer was, and importantly, where she was.

Phase 4
On Raising Funds and Evolving

As our marketing efforts had grown our business so significantly and so quickly, we entered yet another new phase of change and learning. This time, both we and the world around us needed to evolve yet again to move forward.

CHAPTER 10
CAN WE PLEASE MOVE THE STATUS QUO? THANKS.

Australia was very new to developing online retail when we started out in 2009, but, a few years in, Australian consumers were showing that they truly had no fear around buying online. I had read in various news articles that Australia, despite having a relatively small population, was the second-biggest market for both Net-a-Porter and ASOS.com.

Unlike in the United States, Australia did not have an existing culture of catalogue buying so there wasn't a solid process or standard already in place for purchasing something and having it delivered to your door. There were no suppliers for online image photography, for example. We were all figuring out by trial and error what e-commerce best practice was.

There also wasn't an established, accessible ecosystem for entrepreneurs. Venture capital funds were few and far between, and at the time their cheque size and valuations were known to be typically lower than that of their US counterparts. There weren't yet co-working spaces, incubators or much in the way of fostering entrepreneurs at the seed stage.

So we needed to build and figure out everything for ourselves—we needed to move forward without a map. We read books, we watched videos online, we read blogs. We talked to people with expertise in the areas where we felt we needed help.

One of the places where the Australian system needed to catch up to support this new e-commerce economy was in our banking system, which didn't currently treat starting an online business and the associated global transactions as normal.

National Australia Bank was the only bank that was able to provide us with the ability to accept multiple currencies, but opening accounts with them was a huge drain on our already lean resources. We were required to submit business plans in a form that they prescribed to us, we had to place a large deposit of cash into the account, provide personal guarantees, pay significant fees and, on top of all that, there was absolutely no fraud protection. PayPal had recently entered the market and we were using their services. They were facing regulatory issues that neatly aligned with what we were struggling with: the current regulations, government grants and so on only supported offline retail, not e-commerce. Similarly, the banking regulations didn't contemplate a product or service that sat between banks and consumers. This meant that we were both stuck in a situation where we were being regulated in ways that simply didn't make sense and were really holding back development of our industries.

Paul Greenberg had been a client of Mike's at Google. The co-founder of one of the first major e-commerce businesses in Australia and commonly referred to as the grandfather of Australian online retail, Paul proclaimed himself my proud Jewish mother (which I love), and was someone whose advice we sought often. He is the best of people and I cannot tell you enough how wonderful it was to come up in an industry in his footsteps. Paul gathered Vahid Ta'eed—co-founder of Envato, a subscription service for downloadable digital assets for projects—some of the global team from PayPal and me together to lobby federal parliament to see the future economy we were building, and to support it.

I was nervous about the meetings. I had not been paying attention to politics, so I felt many paces behind. Before the meetings I spent my evenings reading about each person we were meeting with. I prepared myself dossiers with their bios, their position on each of the issues connected to our discussion points, their party's position and actions on these points in the past, and a quick review of their most recent work. The last page of my dossier was a list of my asks. (Perhaps my lawyering days did have some practical value.)

Being an ex-lawyer and now co-founder of a fashion tech company, I really thought hard about my outfit. The political circles in Canberra were typically highly conservative in dress. So I wore a high-waisted pencil skirt with straps and a blazer—both of which I had designed—a white button-down shirt, and red Mary Jane–style patent leather stilettos. I wanted to look conservative, yet true to my brand. As we passed through the security checks of Parliament House my red patent leather pumps rolled along the conveyor belt into screening alongside a lineup of black leather oxfords and low, wide-heeled pumps.

We walked into Malcolm Turnbull's office, at the time Shadow Minister for Broadband, Communications and the Digital Economy, who later went on to become prime minister. He quietly regarded each of us as we walked in, before looking down at my feet and without missing a beat saying, 'You must be Jodie Fox'. I'd been so excited to meet him, knowing his business background and feeling that he would be one of the best people to understand our point of view. The meeting was succinct—the man had laser focus. Soon we were off to meet with the remaining ministers on our list.

Our next meeting was with Bruce Billson, Minister for Small Business at the time. As our meeting with Billson was coming to an end, he turned to our group and asked, 'What would you do if you were prime minister for a day?' Everyone was quiet. I looked around the table, pulled my list of asks from my dossier, slid it across the table to him and said, 'I'm glad you asked. May I take you through this?' The energy at the table transformed from formal, sober faces into grins, and Bruce's face opened into a smile. He clearly hadn't expected anyone to actually be prepared for that question, and no-one was—except for me. On the next page is what I put on my list.

– Grants. At the time, eligibility threshold requirements for the majority of business grants were impossible for many small online businesses to meet. For example, Commercialisation Australia's requirement of a patentable concept or strong design was impractical for many small businesses. Yet, those businesses might have many other reasons that they could not be easily copied.

– Education. For Australians to become global online business leaders, change must start in the education system. Subjects taught in business school must incorporate better online business instruction so that this is a natural aspect of business in the minds of tomorrow's businesspeople. Further, we should also encourage more students to study software engineering with a view to producing more and better digital minds domestically. It goes hand-in-hand to say that it is important that innovative Australian online businesses have the support to grow into global leaders, as it will be their task to become big enough and interesting enough to keep these graduates in the country.

- Postal services. This was often the most difficult part of our customer experience; our postal services were below par, particularly internationally.

- Goods and Services Tax. This issue had prompted a productivity inquiry with respect to whether it should be applied to imported goods. (The issue has arisen again since then, most recently dropping the price threshold on imported goods that attract GST. I suspect this will continue to be discussed in the future.)

- Banking regulation. Banking options available to small businesses in Australia were often financially onerous and time consuming to set up and maintain. We loved using PayPal because it circumvented the majority of these issues and helped Shoes of Prey to grow more quickly than we could have otherwise. There was a need for regulation reform so that there is room for more innovative banking solutions for small businesses.

The discussions were positive and seeded some clear paths to change.

And I had found my voice in a room that I never imagined I could.

In the lead-up to the meetings, Mike and Michael had questioned me for spending time outside the office preparing for the meetings, rather than resting up to be rejuvenated for Shoes of Prey the next day (or, since I was already working, simply dedicate that additional time to the Shoes of Prey business). But I knew that the preparation I'd made had completely paid off.

I learned that when I am fully prepared or briefed and understand my situation from a grassroots level, I carry myself with confidence, grace and intelligence. Spending time preparing would be my secret weapon to prepare for much bigger meetings to come.

It was so much fun to ride these highs of personal and professional wins. Who ever imagined I would have the chance to have a voice at Parliament House? And I'd learned an important lesson about how I performed best. Yet the highs were fleeting against the day-to-day learning by doing.

No personal space

Michael and I never really worried too much about starting a company together. Not nearly as much as those around us did. Some worried about the viability of the company if we broke up. Some worried about the viability of the company if we stayed together! They thought ahead about the natural life stages we would go through together (what if we had babies? Or took holidays together?). Some worried about us jointly holding a large stake in the company and voting as a bloc.

We were both really positive people and hadn't even suspected that it might not work. There were so many amazing things to appreciate. For example, so few partners really get to see each other in full flight professionally. Every day we were in meetings together and when meetings were going well I'd want to high-five Michael and tell him how well he was doing.

On the other hand, it became more and more challenging to relax around one another. If I had decided to rest and I heard Michael tapping away on his keyboard, a sense of guilt would rise in me that I couldn't ignore. At first it came out just as frustration with him, but I had to find ways to own this, and get comfortable with this new normal. This normal was gruelling. We'd fall asleep under our laptops and wake to pick them up from where they'd slid off the bed and start working again immediately on waking. Michael and I started travelling to China more frequently, and not always together, which made for weeks or months of separation.

And finally, in the summer of 2011, The Campaign Palace needed to take back the space we'd been working from. So our office of eight, along with a few hundred pairs of shoes, started operating from our one-bedroom apartment in Surry Hills, Sydney. During a 40-degree Celsius heat wave. With no air conditioning. It really was almost too much. But when you're in the middle of building something you truly believe in and are so focused on, nothing really feels like too much to give — which is both good and bad.

We seated six people at our large wooden dining table; it was the desk space for those who had desktop computers that weren't portable. I also had an outdoor setting that seated four people (six people at a stretch). This became the lunch room, and the work station for the two team members who didn't fit at the dining table.

Working from the dinner table.

For a three-month period we searched for a new office space from the sweltering apartment. I'd send my team home when the temperatures got too high and would continue to burrow away at my tasks as my sweat dripped onto the keyboard. The bathroom wasn't really up to what was being asked of it, and one of our engineers was allergic to something in the apartment, but he still diligently turned up to his 'desk' (my kitchen table), sneezing intermittently.

Despite the team being as considerate as they could be, I completely lost my privacy. Michael had gone to China for this period, so I was hosting the team alone. As just a matter of course, everyone became familiar with where everything was in our apartment. Arrivals to 'the office' started as early as 8 am, occasionally earlier, and people started to leave somewhere around 5.30 or 6 pm at the earliest. There was literally no way for me to take a sick day if I needed to over that period of time; my bedroom adjoined the small but open lounge/dining/living area that was now entirely given over to office space.

I noticed my furniture and rugs becoming worn very quickly. But, more than that, my mental health was becoming worn with the constant focus and connection to work.

We looked at so many office spaces. Most needed pretty significant renovations, and we didn't want to spend the time putting our focus on anything but running the business.

We finally found an office space that happened to be literally one block from our apartment. It was new and cool, with polished concrete, breakout areas and well-placed graffiti. As we prepared to move into the space we began to advertise additional roles. Growth had been steady and it was time to step up.

We interviewed new hires ahead of moving into the new office space, and conducted them from a café close to my apartment. Unfortunately this was not foolproof. The café wifi dropped out with reasonable consistency, so if we had Michael dialled in for any part of the interview, I'd be forced to apologetically move the remainder of the interview to the apartment, among the chaos. It still stuns me that people agreed to work for us under these circumstances.

Learning how to interview

I realised I was interviewing without a lot of experience as an interviewer, so I sat down to research and map out what I was looking for in these interviews. I settled on the below principles, and they haven't really changed:

Are they a brilliant jerk?

We were always looking for brilliant people, but not at the expense of our culture. The concept of the brilliant jerk has been well documented over the years, and in many ways the title speaks for itself, so I won't elaborate here. The key reason I didn't want a jerk, no matter how brilliant, is that they'd probably demotivate everyone else, which is an enormous resource cost and a retention issue.

I'd try to get a gauge on this by asking teamwork questions.

Do they care about working here?

Passion for the company is so underrated. I think it's a really defensible strategy, because when you care you will go the extra mile. You will unpack problems in a more thorough way. If you're passionate because you are also the customer of the brand, you will be very likely to be able to identify or relate to pain points that will lead to innovation.

To find this out I'd ask a pretty simple question — 'Why do you want to work for Shoes of Prey?'

What are they passionate about? Does it align with the role they've applied for?

It's really difficult to get someone focused and motivated if the role is not something that they want to do. This is really tricky to balance — I've seen people apply for roles just to get into a company and then find their time there miserable. It's really important to get to the heart of what their ideal role is to make sure it aligns with what they're applying for. It's not to discount the fact that people might move around within your company later on; it's just to make sure you're getting the right person on board.

I normally get to this by asking something like 'What is your dream job?'

Proof of knowledge

This is so very tough to prove. At Shoes of Prey, we often set a task as part of the interview process and sometimes even had the candidate come in for a trial day. I personally haven't found a better way to get to the bottom of this.

(continued)

Learning how to interview (*cont'd*)

If you're completing a task for an interview process, remember that timeliness is something we looked at as an indication of enthusiasm about the role.

This is the most important question. Cultural fit is as important as knowing if the person you're hiring has the skills they need to do the job. If you don't really like someone, you're probably not going to get good work done with them. This goes both ways. If there's discomfort on either end, that's definitely something to keep in mind.

Overall, I learned three key principles that I still interview by today:

1. Always test claimed skills and knowledge with a practical test.

2. Cultural fit and engagement wins over brilliance.

3. Always hire with a three-month probation period — this is when you really validate the above findings.

Setting up the new office consumed a huge amount of my time. We had got access to the space just days before we'd planned to move our new team into it and, alongside these new starters, we had our business partner arriving from the Netherlands on the day the office opened.

We moved desks in, ran cabling and I waited nervously for a very delayed electricity company approval to arrive on the Friday afternoon. It was illegal for our power to go on without it. Joe, the electrician was literally standing by the electricity box with me, waiting for the call or email. And at 4.55pm, it arrived. I hugged Joe, the burly Eastern European man who had watched me bite my nails for the past hour, and ran up to the office. It was an unorganised mess. I had to set it up over the weekend. But I didn't care, I reached over, and flipped on the light switch. The fluorescent tubes blinked to life and I sat on the floor and smiled.

CHAPTER 11
THINGS YOU CAN CONTROL AND THINGS YOU CANNOT

Every step of the journey presented unmappable decisions that initially felt too overwhelmingly large to consider. However, in accepting imperfection in our solutions, with a view to continually improve — as we had from the day we launched the company — we made the overwhelming manageable, and the manageable eventually simple.

Work–life balance in the early years

Marc Andreesen has an amazing quote that crystallises the insanity of the entrepreneurial journey. He describes the daily unmapped journey as an 'emotional rollercoaster'. It really captures where we are in this story up to this moment here. And we haven't even got to the really good bits yet.

The tricky thing is that while I was on the Shoes of Prey journey, particularly early on, balance was nice in theory but didn't mean anything in practice. I'd get so immersed in things I was doing that I would forget to eat, and sleep only four hours a night. I didn't stop to think about anything other than the tasks at hand.

Just prior to starting Shoes of Prey I'd started to experience what I can only describe as a private kind of hell. I'd been through periods of irrationally heavy worries and panic as a child, but it had begun to return in a much more powerful adult form. At the time I couldn't work out what seem like obvious causes in hindsight — a marriage that was unhappy, and struggling to find an identity in a world where I just didn't know what I wanted. (Remember, at this time I had just transitioned from law to advertising and then into Shoes of Prey, still exploring if this was the right path.)

It manifested in episodes of severe nausea, fever and dizziness that drove me to find the nearest cold surface to cool my fever and a private place to throw up. These had started when I was 14, and had increased in both severity and frequency from 2007 onward. At the time I had no idea that these had a name: panic attacks. I thought something might be really wrong with me. Was something attacking my system, slowly breaking it down? Or had I just eaten something bad? I cannot tell you how many bathroom floors I have graced in a lather of panicked sweat over the years, and some days (though much less frequently now) still do.

We were now in our cool new office, and had been settled there for about a year. I'd had multiple burnout moments that would stop me for a period of one to three days. This burnout looked like a very severe cold, or a kind of debilitating nausea that took over. After these episodes I'd feel somewhat sobered and … get right up and go back to it again.

Things got messy sometimes. I remember a day when I was in my office working with Anna and Luke, the founders and designers of the label Romance Was Born, on shoes for their next runway show. It was one of my favourite things to do, and I was so excited to work with them; their designs were always so avant-garde and beautiful. It was a dream to collaborate and bring to life shoes that came from the realms of their imagination. Now, taking a step back from the glamour, I'd had the most excruciating toothache for two days and, while I knew I really needed to get to the dentist, I just didn't have time. I messaged my assistant, DaveDave (he'd earned this nickname when, while traveling with friends, he demonstrated the most incredible organisational skills that they duplicated his name in reference to the navigation tool, TomTom), while I was in the meeting and asked him to please go to the chemist and buy the strongest painkiller they'd sell him and to discreetly let me know when he was back so I could pop out of the meeting to take it. And if it was okay … Would he also please book me a dentist appointment?

I finally wanted something to change. As part of my attempt to distribute my focus and interests beyond the office, I planted a vegetable garden in our courtyard and Michael offered to buy me a cat for my birthday. We were in the thick of working on our relationship, and at a point where we were coming to terms with the fact that we might not stay together. 'Fixing' anything we could that was adding to the pressures on our relationship was of utmost importance, and maybe, just maybe, having something important outside of work would help. The idea was that these were things I couldn't ignore — their very survival depended on me. I planted rosemary, sage, basil, thyme, mint, rocket, tomatoes, strawberries, eggplants and beans. I found that I loved doing something so physical. The smell of the dirt, the little joys of seeing something grow from seed. And the flavour of freshly-picked herbs really cannot be beaten.

Working with your hands

Find something to do with your hands that takes you right out of your working day. I've tried so many things over the years, and, honestly, they have all worked; just some more consistently than others. Some of the things I've tried have included:

- committing to always cook dinner after work: the acts of chopping, stirring, timing — all of it just made me transition from the work day to my home environment
- making ceramics — just shaping something from a lump of clay into an ugly cup or vase feels so fantastic
- gardening
- swimming in the ocean.

The key theme here for me is to spend time with no screens, doing something really practical.

It took a while for me to find my cat, but when I met her, I knew. She was a little lilac British shorthair who purred instantly in my arms. The seller warned me off of her, saying she was moody — but I didn't believe it. I felt connected to this little ball of fur when I held her. And so she came home with us. You might remember that the origins of the name 'Shoes of Prey' were in the idea that women *hunt* fashion. And so my little cat's name was Hunter.

Hunter hard at work at Shoes of Prey.

Of course, now that I had a game plan for improvements in my personal life, other things were going awry with the business.

You're only as good as your third parties

Our orders were increasing, we'd settled into our new office ... and we'd started to receive complaints about customers receiving shoes with dents and scratches. We couldn't understand how this was happening. We added more tissue paper, and looked for sturdy outer-cartons to add more protection. While we ascertained from our customers that it wasn't a shoe quality issue from our production process, it was still producing the same end result ... customers receiving damaged product.

Shipping shape

We asked our customers to send us photos of the products they received so we could better understand the problem. When we saw picture after picture of taped-up, mangled shoeboxes, we realised that the freighter we were using, who was charging us by volume on receipt of our shoeboxes, would open them, cut inches off the height of the boxes, and then tape them up and ship them, creating a much lower volume than they were charging us for and damaging both our products and reputation along the way.

When you first think about shipping, it seems like a really simple project: choose a provider, pack the goods and send them to your customer.

But it's not.

We tested out postal-based services (the postal systems run in each local country, usually government run), only to find that as soon as the goods arrived in the destination country they would be handed over to the domestic postal service, which did not use the original tracking number. Sometimes shoes would go missing for weeks, or never show up at all, and we couldn't find out what had happened.

Ultimately (and eventually!) we found that DHL was our best option worldwide. Products were trackable end-to-end, customers could reschedule missed deliveries and the products were delivered anywhere in the world on an average of four days from the shoes leaving the factory.

In hindsight I wish we'd tested shipping providers during our beta testing period. And I wish we hadn't taken for granted any of the features that I'd just thought were normal for any shipping service. I'd never imagined I'd need to ask if packages were ever opened and altered by the shipper. (Admittedly I'm not sure we could have ever known that we'd need to ask this until experiencing it.) And I'd never thought that tracking numbers would just stop working.

But it really pushed me to ask the detailed questions and look for ways to test third-party providers before plugging them into our entire business. At the outset this is much harder to do because momentum is more critical than perfection, but I do believe that finding even small ways to test is worth it in the long run.

A cautionary tale on packaging

As our sales increased with our marketing activity, our post-sales approach was something people not only talked about, but shared. Our very first shoes didn't have great packaging. We simply used the same light-green boxes that our supplier used. Any information that was important to the order was written on the side of the box in ballpoint pen, often in Chinese characters. Again, momentum was more important than perfection, but now it was time to improve this aspect of our product.

I'd long cherished the experiences I had as a consumer when the packaging of a product was special. It really heightened the relationship I had with the brand, and my sense of how much I liked the product itself. Because we were a brand that brought your design to life, I felt that we had a really special role to play in the unveiling of your design in real life, when it finally arrived in your hands.

And, because we were mostly online, we rarely got to be a physical part of the customer's experience with us. This was the one way, in a very pertinent moment, that we could add to and be part of their experience.

I'd seen the rave reviews of Net-a-Porter's packaging: a black box with white, stitched-edge grosgrain ribbon. The swaths of black tissue enrobing the clothing seemed so dreamy to me. Given my budget restrictions I wasn't a Net-a-Porter customer, but I wanted to see what everyone was talking about. So I found an Alexander Wang T-shirt that was within budget (and still in my wardrobe today). The physical experience was as awesome as I had read about. And so I turned my mind to how we'd build our own version of this.

Given our branding, black shoeboxes and black tissue paper made sense for us too. I had our logo embossed in gold on the shoebox, and when you lifted the lid, there would be a thick black bow for you to undo, revealing the gold shoe-shaped sticker that held the tissue paper in place. Beneath the tissue paper, the shoes were nestled in our very own branded shoe bags. (I assessed a number of textures before finally choosing the materials for these.) We also included heel grips, toe pads, a photo of your shoes that you could stick to the box (so you could see what shoes were in that box when they were stored), and a handwritten letter.

As we shipped more shoes with this new packaging, people filmed and photographed their 'unboxing' and posted it to their social media without our encouragement, resulting in a halo effect on our sales.

Still, I kept thinking about the shoebox. Shoeboxes really took up a lot of space, but they were the best way to store shoes. I lived in a reasonably small apartment and found it difficult to store my shoes well. I wondered if we designed the shoeboxes to function like drawers that could be stacked or connected together, we might solve a problem for myself and other women. The shoeboxes connected together, over time, would become their own neat furniture solution for the storage of shoes.

I sketched out a drawer-shaped shoebox with a little ribbon pull tag on the drawer. The inside was padded with foam and lined with black satin—a beautiful experience, and a great way to store shoes well. I sat with our shoebox supplier and worked through the design explanation. Then I crossed my fingers and waited.

The samples arrived and a few weeks later we started to send shoes out in their new packaging. I was excited. I felt that I'd created an innovation in shoe packaging that really solved a problem I related to!

Emails started to come in from our customers. But they weren't the emails I'd wanted.

The shoeboxes were being squashed in transit, and in their new squashed shape the drawer wouldn't open, trapping the customers' shoes inside. Customers were resorting to wrestling their shoes out or taking to the shoebox with scissors and box cutters—which was very far from the experience we'd intended.

Rather than adding to the elevated experience we'd created for our customers, I'd created a messy hassle. *That* I really should have tested before rolling out to the entire business.

CHAPTER 12
THE MONEY QUESTION

Whenever I'm out and about, I always look at the stores I walk past and feel so surprised and impressed by how many people have started businesses on their own. Dry cleaners, convenience stores, pharmacies, boutiques — it's really extraordinary. And they are important to the fabric of our communities. I was recently in my hometown for Christmas and bumped into one of the ladies I used to buy snacks from after school. I say snacks because other kids bought lollies. I used to buy a fresh bread roll and antipasti. She still remembered me and I still remembered her — Norma. Her face was as much a part of my school years as that of any teacher or friend, and I am so grateful to have that kind of history in my life.

However, you don't often read about these kinds of businesses. Newspapers always tell the sexy stories of businesses that are trying to be unicorns (billion-dollar startups). But it's not necessary to aim for this if it's not what you want. You can have a really successful business and a great life without pursuing that path.

In 2011 we were at a stage in the company where we were growing fast, and we were profitable, but, given the opportunity, we wanted to grow much more quickly. Companies in this kind of situation generally have two options:

1.   to bootstrap and try to get by on just what they make, or

2.   to raise funds.

But first, what's Bootstrapping? It's getting yourself into (or out of) a situation using only the resources you already have. So in this case, only with the money, time and people power that you already have.

And second, what's fundraising? It's bringing cash into the business from an outside source to make things grow faster than you would without it.

Ok. Now back to my bootstrapping vs fundraising dilemma.

I'm seriously torn on my views with respect to bootstrapping or raising funds. With the greatest of generalisations, fundraising is difficult because, to do it, you need to have very aggressive company goals, along with the strategy and ability to deliver on them. Otherwise investors won't want to sign up. And in my opinion, there is a big difference between the way you run a company to achieve a new round of funds and the way you run a company to achieve sustainable profitability. When you raise funds, you're expected to spend the dollars you have in the bank to grow and scale quickly. Profit comes much later than it might in a bootstrapped business. But this constant focus on the next round of fundraising can become a very tricky cycle to manage.

If you haven't been through the process of raising funds, it can seem like an absolute mystery. So I'm going to do my best to share my experience with it and the way I think about it. I've put more detailed notes on the topic in appendix C, just in case it's something you want to think about in more detail.

Raising capital

As co-founders, we had always agreed and committed to the vision that we wanted Shoes of Prey to be a large, global company. None of us were there to build a business that would only provide a comfortable lifestyle. Our vision and data convinced us that the concept of Shoes of Prey had the potential to scale. In establishing this focus so early on we were able to ensure that our passion and ambition were built on substance. This predisposed us to raising capital.

At Shoes of Prey we were initially happy with bootstrapping. This was because we didn't believe we were at a stage that would attract investment that we would find interesting. Until I took a call with a French banker in London. We spoke for almost an hour and I shared our numbers with him during the conversation. He thought we could raise around £2 million. This was exactly the kind of number that would be interesting for us, so we turned our minds to it more seriously.

We coincidentally had an inbound call from two girls in Paris who wanted to roll out Shoes of Prey in France. This joint venture didn't progress because they actually wanted to start their own brand on top of our infrastructure. And with a little digging I found that they were connected to the banker who had called us. I immediately revoked his access to our numbers. He was not progressing discussions with us on funding and, while his call had sparked this path for us, it felt clear that his intentions may not have been the same as ours.

We began speaking with multiple venture capital funds and high net worth individuals. We mined our personal and professional networks for contacts of potential investors.

Our first round

Some of our first investors came from making friends with Rebekah Campbell at Posse (a place where bands could connect with their fanbase), whose office was just down the hallway from ours. She introduced us to her investors when they came to her office for meetings. This is how we met Rick Baker, who was at MLC then and is now one of the founding partners of Blackbird Ventures, and the tech investment titan Bill Tai, among others.

Our first round took a lot of time and effort to get off the ground. I think in hindsight, aside from having no idea about what we were doing, this happened because:

- *We were unproven.* While we each had solid career backgrounds, we were all still reasonably young (27, 28) and had not started, let alone run, our own businesses before.

- *The idea was unproven.* While we had acquired customers and broken even, this was still a novel concept — could it truly find market fit in the global mass-market?

Our pitch

To prove we were the right team and this was the right idea, we had to counter all of this in a very compelling pitch deck. At a high level it covered the following areas.

The problem we solved that other companies couldn't

We wanted to show that Shoes of Prey worked to solve a problem in the market. To do this, we focused on two key areas:

- *Sizing.* Most shoe labels only offered sizes from an Australian 5.5 to 10.5. We could offer sizes 2.5 to 15, including the ability to make one shoe a different size to the other, and to accommodate width adjustments. We estimated that people with this need accounted for around 16 per cent of the market.

- *Special occasion shoes.* Specifically, weddings. Brides had a fairly narrow selection of shoes available to them and were willing to spend more on their wedding day. We could offer special shoes for that special day in a way that simply didn't seem to exist (think blue shoe lining, messaging embossed into the shoe, and so on).

The unit economics and size of the opportunity

Specific unit economics were always a challenge for us, given that each shoe was custom made. However, we were able to use averages to show that selling pairs of shoes was not only profit generating, but that we could increase our profit margins over time. To demonstrate just how big the market opportunity could be, we corroborated a series of data points including:

- The size of the women's footwear market in the USA (excluding athletic shoes)

  - forecast for 2013 global footwear market was US$238 billion.

  - forecast for 2013 global women's dress and casual footwear market was US$84 billion.

  - market was forecast to grow annually at 7 per cent.

- The only other footwear customisation business that we felt had broken ground, NIKEiD (now Nike By You), we understood to have grown to US$100 million per year as of 2010.

- The size of other women's footwear businesses that had raised funding, such as Jimmy Choo, which in 2011 had annual sales of US$233 million and had sold to Labelux for US$811 million in May 2011.

Our credentials as a team

We felt that the way we sold ourselves as a team would give us the highest possibility of succeeding in this venture. Our credentials included our differentiated but complimentary backgrounds. Mike studied law and IT, Michael studied law and commerce, and I studied law and international business. After university, Mike went on to work at Google as a software engineer, Michael went on to work at a really fast growing retailer before going to Google, and I went on to learn about building brands working in advertising. I was also (obviously?) pretty excited about being able to design my own shoes.

We also had such different personalities, and we thought about issues really differently. I will admit that this did cause tension at times, but overall it was a really good thing. The reason that the tension was never the reason for a breakdown was that we always worked on a premise of totally believing in what we were doing and in each other. And, we had a close but very frank, honest friendship built on a lot of trust.

Much of proving our credentials came from spending time with the people who were considering investing in us.

How we would spend the money

Knowing what we would spend the money on, how much growth it could create and how long we expected that money to last before we would either be profitable, or need to raise more funds was critical. Broadly, the areas we wanted to spend this money were:

- *Hiring people.* We'd probably spend money on key hires that are revenue generating, that is, people who could really grow our business. In particular, hiring a more robust marketing team.

- *Equipment.* We would need to develop software and potentially buy machinery. Later we would look at opening stores (covered in chapter 15), which would also need significant investment.

- *Marketing.* We wanted to test more avenues and invest more in channels that were working well for us. We also needed to start investing more in the lifetime value of our customers (as in, repeat sales).

- *Addressing consumer data.* We had surveyed our market, ran focus groups and found from our research that to convert the mass-market into customers, we needed to do four key things:
  - Reduce lead times to under 2 weeks.
  - Simplify the shoe design experience.
  - Remove a premium for customisation.
  - Establish distribution where the mass market fashion customer shops.

We'd also had to build out our view on the valuation of the company, and how much of the company we would be willing to sell to raise funds. We didn't typically include this in the pitch deck, but would speak about it as a matter of course in the meetings. We had also agreed how much of the company we were willing to part with for investment. The primary goal was retaining control with the founding team.

Keeping the momentum

Once we had connected with investors and given our pitch, we kept up our momentum. Michael was the key contact for investors and did a great job of replying quickly to detailed questions that would come through and following up for feedback and responses to our pitch.

Answering *all* the questions — especially the ones they didn't ask

I do remember during the fundraising process being lightly questioned about Michael and I being married. We posed a risk to investors that had to be considered. What if we broke up? What if we fought badly with one another? However, the questions came and went, and it didn't seem to be a barrier to raising capital.

When we were pitching, the majority of venture capitalists were men. They didn't understand why *anyone* would want to design their own shoes. But the majority of their assistants, who set up our meetings, were women. We had them design shoes, and had the shoes arrive to them the day before or day of our meeting. The response was almost always exciting and provided the venture capitalist with the context that a female in our target audience naturally possessed.

Ultimately, in our first round of funding, we raised just over A$2 million. One of the key learnings from this experience was that we just needed to get one investor to offer a term sheet to us (a list of the terms on which they'd be willing to invest in you). After that, it really was a lot like a game of dominos. It took just one person to say 'yes' for the rest to feel confident too.

And along with the money in the bank, we formed our first formal board.

Board seats were normally negotiated by the shareholders. Larger shareholders would often request a seat of their own as a condition of the funding. On the board we initially had two shareholders, all three co-founders and an independent board member. We also encouraged all shareholders to attend board meetings as they were available to.

Staying human

Over the years of pitching, we gained a clearer understanding of the process, the terminology and the pressure points venture capitalists were most interested in understanding. And, our pitching became more and more polished. But, never less human. I will never forget one of my early meetings in Los Angeles with Elaine Stead and Ben Dunphy, who were considering investing in us with the fund they worked for, Blue Sky. It would be for our fifth raise, of US$15 million. We met at a local Mexican restaurant, Mercado. I had flown in from another location that morning, worked the day, given a speech at a local startup night, and then come to join them at the restaurant along with Michael. Exhausted, I excused myself from partaking in margaritas and got stuck into the guacamole. We chatted for hours. Things seemed to go well, and eventually it was time to leave. I was the last to get up from the table and we filed one by one down a narrow staircase to the exit of the restaurant. Well, at least they did. I managed to catch the first step and fall down the remaining stairs in a series of loud thuds, but surprisingly no swearing. Shocked, I stood myself up and put my game face on. I walked around the corner to face a concerned chorus of 'are you okay?'

'Sure, yes, I'm fine,' I lied. I was embarrassed, lightheaded and in a lot of pain. We waited outside for our Ubers to arrive, and I kept up the facade until I came so close to fainting that I had to give it up and crouch down into a sitting position. Thankfully the team were whisked away in their Ubers momentarily. I got back to the Airbnb and with nothing but Mickey Mouse bandaids at my disposal, I taped up what would turn out to be a couple of fractured fingers.

(For the record, we did end up landing the funding.)

Occasionally, there's a really awkward pitch

I was invited to a business meeting at a bar with a potential investor for Shoes of Prey. I didn't love the idea of meeting in a bar, but it's also not unheard of. So I went.

I hadn't met this person before. When I walked in and we spotted each other, the first thing he said to me wasn't 'It's great to meet you Jodie', or even just 'Hello' — it was 'You look amazing'.

Let me start by saying that I don't know that he really meant to say this. And we did have a good meeting, but I did feel just a little bit awkward. Sometimes it's hard to tell if someone is being friendly and awkward, or if they have ulterior motives.

Of course, if we were meeting socially then this may have landed differently. But this was so clearly meant to be a business meeting. This opening line, mixed with him having set the meeting at a bar, mixed with him not really talking about what we were there for, mixed with him being in a position of power ... it made for a bit of an uncomfortable and awkward situation.

I think earlier in my career I would have dismissed this as an off-the-cuff comment. But it really sat on my mind. Over the years I've seen how what can be seemingly innocuous comments contribute to a gender bias that really affects women's professional opportunities. A better opening compliment would have been something like 'Great work on Shoes of Prey' ... something that wouldn't have been out of place being said to me or my male co-founders.

I brushed off the awkwardness and we got through the rest of the meeting without a hitch. But the discomfort of the start of the evening stuck with me. I'd started a YouTube channel where I would share snippets of our journey, new product launches, answer questions and pose questions I was trying to answer in the business. I decided to make a video on the topic. And I did it for a number of reasons:

- I personally believe that the vast majority of people don't want to be creepy and awkward. But, if you accuse them of that, it just creates embarrassment and a huge divide that's difficult to cross. If we instead have a blame-free conversation about how certain words and actions are received versus how they are intended, well, then there's a chance of understanding each other and making change.

- I don't really think he meant to say what he did, and I wish I'd found a way to help him have a better meeting opening line next time.

- I didn't think I'd be able to think of every important aspect of this topic by myself, so I wanted to gather other opinions.

And it led to a really great conversation. The video was picked up, recut and circulated by both *The Guardian* and *Al Jazeera*, and the hashtag #canhesaythat started trending. Here is a summary of the outtakes from that conversation:

- Giving a compliment is okay, but it's not okay to talk about appearance as the first interaction in a business meeting.

- If the appearance comment had been at least connected to the meeting it may have worked—in other words, these two options suggested by a commenter named treetopy: 'You look so vibrant for having traveled. What's your secret?'…. or maybe, 'Great ensemble … are those Shoes of Prey pumps?'

- Probably better not to agree to meetings in a bar! The setting itself was something I could have taken control of with something simple like saying I wasn't available at that time, and moving the meeting to the morning, over coffee.

- Sometimes it can be a cultural issue—a friend of mine who is Italian said 'That depends if he's Italian … we're just told to always compliment a woman'.

- Context is important—women founders fundraising are rare (I think the figure in the United States is that only 8 per cent of funded startups have female founders) and for the most part VCs are men. It's a new situation, so we probably all need a little more experience to understand what works and what doesn't.

- Men receive a lot of mixed messages from society, media and women in their lives as to whether they should compliment, socialise or be formal. Let's keep having open and blame-free discussions to make these messages clear when it comes to business.

- Being nice doesn't mean accepting everything directed your way. It does give you the chance to approach tough conversations in a way that's productive and impactful.

All of this was pre #metoo, which has unearthed this conversation in a very powerful way. There are very obvious and awful cases where both men and women have been subjected to completely unacceptable behaviour. Separately, there is momentum for us to reset the norms of day-to-day language and behaviour that's corrosive to gender equality. And I still believe today that blame-free conversations that seek to share and educate will get us to this place the fastest.

PHASE 5
ON ESTABLISHMENT AND TENACITY

With funding on board and a growing team, our systems and processes needed to be properly established to support us as we moved to scale. Our manufacturing was unstable and our people policies were understood but not written down. And, Michael and I needed to decide if we would remain husband and wife co-founders, or become simply co-founders.

CHAPTER 13
GROWING IN CHINA

In 2011 both our business in Australia and the China team had grown. We had moved from our first China office and away from the little boy across the road. By the time we moved, he had grown to a little boy chattering happily, wielding his toys and making his family laugh. I could see myself in this little boy. While he had grown from baby to toddler, I had grown from a confused and nervous baby entrepreneur to one who just might find her feet, any day now.

We'd set up our new China office and small team inside some available space in our main supplier's factory, which had some clear benefits: we were connected to existing infrastructure, able to check on shoe orders quickly, and there was no freight time or cost from the supplier to us. This was all really positive — until it wasn't, which I'll get to later.

The business was growing reasonably quickly and we'd come to the conclusion that we needed someone in a management role, on the ground, full-time in China. A law school friend of Michael's was considering a career change, and we thought he'd be a great fit. Brendan was incredibly intelligent, fearless when it came to the unknown and fluent in Mandarin. And, he has some of the best comedic timing I've ever witnessed in real life.

You may notice that I haven't listed his qualifications in manufacturing shoes. That was because he didn't have any. We didn't have strong networks in those areas in those days and, besides, we were really focused on recruiting intelligent generalists to our team. The fact that he could also break down the language and cultural barrier was incredibly exciting.

Brendan joined our team in Sydney and initially trained with our Customer Happiness team to learn about the issues affecting our customers that might be solved with improving our supply chain.

The thing about on-demand manufacturing

Before Brendan reached China, small cracks had started to appear in our relationship with our suppliers. It may seem odd, given that our volumes were increasing, but let me explain. Normally, larger orders do mean a better relationship with your supplier. But in our case, it did not. We were applying pressure to systems and processes that still found their highest efficiencies (and profitability) in mass production: making a large number of the exact same item, not a large number of unique items.

Let me give an example to help this make sense. Very generally speaking, when you reach the stage of putting all the pieces of the shoe together, it's called 'lasting' the shoe. Normally, a mass-production factory will spend a couple of hours setting up their lasting machine for one particular style, and then last only that style of shoe that day, and maybe even for the following weeks. Whereas we required multiple different last settings a day, which was challenging for the factory to optimise for with their existing systems and processes.

It meant that our cost of making shoes was generally much higher than that of mass-produced shoes. This is partly why our shoes weren't mass-market prices. (The other reason is that the shoes were much higher quality than mass-market shoes.)

It also meant that shoe production was becoming much more difficult, rather than easier, dealing with more of these one-off, high-touch orders. And the real money for these factories was in volume, so our orders were being deprioritised. Delivery was slowing down instead of speeding up, and errors were becoming more frequent. We were enormously frustrated and our customers were showing early signs of frustration too.

It was in this context that Brendan started his time with Shoes of Prey in China. Having been briefed on the issues during the training time he'd spent with us, Brendan began his first week applying some pushback to one of our suppliers—who responded by yelling at Brendan so aggressively that his first check-in report to us back in Sydney at headquarters was that he thought he'd just terminated our relationship with our main supplier.

Of course, it wasn't as bad as he'd feared. (In hindsight I wonder if the supplier was attempting to set a new dynamic with their new point of contact.)

As we now understood that simply pushing harder on our suppliers wouldn't work, we started to develop solutions for bottlenecks that our orders were causing in the process. In a bid to keep our suppliers, we started to assume responsibility for parts of the shoe-making process that they didn't want to undertake. For example, we grew our China team and began to develop our own shoe patterns and pattern system. We even offered our developments to the suppliers to implement into their process, but each time we were met with a no. They weren't interested in this type of research and development; it was peripheral to the core of their business, which was mass manufacturing.

Key metrics we had for our supplier didn't improve, and at times they got worse. Things began to look dire — our customers' impatience was growing. We knew that if we didn't fix our supply chain, there wouldn't be any orders to fill. We needed a factory that had been built and optimised for on-demand production, but it didn't exist. There was something called a Sample Room, which is almost exactly what it sounds like. They are small studios within factories that turn out prototypes, one at a time. But they weren't designed to scale with the kind of volumes we were doing.

While our suppliers did not want to change their systems and processes to deliver as they had promised, they also did not want to lose our business. We were in a tough situation because we had put a huge amount of our supply with just one supplier. (We should have looked at diversifying earlier — however, with the data and resources available to us at the time, it made sense that we took the path we did.)

As time wore on, and we took on more shoe-making processes, we hired more talent with long-term expertise in making shoes. And it seemed like *maybe* starting our own factory was something worth considering and not as far out of reach as it once had been.

Before starting Shoes of Prey, I hadn't really thought too much about how things got made. I just knew that I loved when things were in stock, and loved it even more when they were on sale. I had thought that we were building a retail business; but as we unpacked our supply chain needs, we realised if we didn't solve making one pair of shoes at a time, at scale, we would have to close the doors. It looked like we'd need to get more involved with manufacturing.

As we dug into what it would take to make shoes on demand at scale, I started to see the systemic issues around the pleasure I got when things were available on the shelf. I guess I must have known on some level, but I finally saw the financial and environmental price of what it means to have things in stock. Thousands of items get made and shipped all over the world, in the hope that people will buy them. And, to get the discounts I loved so much — if the items don't sell, they are discounted and eventually, in the worst-case scenario, disposed of.

We started some very early research on the ground, with Brendan quietly putting together his learnings. Some of our China team had relationships with people who worked for our suppliers, and people love to talk; we had to be very discreet. Yet, like all good secrets, it got out. Our supplier became suspicious and agitated. We didn't want to be manufacturers. But we were stuck. If we didn't at least explore becoming our own manufacturer, our whole business might be over. The supplier started to have our people (Brendan in particular) followed. They wanted to know what we were up to. Suppliers of raw elements (materials, heels, etc.) whom we approached to understand the process of buying direct from them would report back to our main supplier, who in turn would express their dismay, clearly and emotionally, to Brendan.

Brendan became the subject of repeated onslaughts of yelling from our main supplier — sometimes from an individual, other times from a group of people. Even the smallest of requests seemed to be explosive: a rejection of a shoe for an obvious quality issue, or the discussion of a certain leather. It was all too much. The discomfort for Brendan's very small team on the ground in China was real, confronting and required huge amounts of personal resilience to weather. Which they did, with a calm and rational approach of which I am still in awe.

But after months of this (stretching into almost a year), the confronting nature of the China team's day-to-day was untenable. Circumstances had to change.

Brendan tells a story of having come away from a particularly trying week. He had finished work at 11.30 pm on a Friday night and had gone out to a bar for dinner and a beer. He'd wanted a Corona, but they only came in buckets of four. He drank two and put the other two in his back pockets as he prepared to leave the bar. There had been a monsoon in the region inflicting days on end of torrential rain that was still falling as he stepped out into the street. He eventually walked into the apartment complex still feeling down about the week and all that had transpired. He felt alone and was low on hope. The drainage of the vast courtyard of the apartment complex had failed under the downpour, and had transformed the tiling into a lake thick with industrial city grime and dirt that had built up under the now inches of water he needed to cross to get home. Traversing the courtyard he slipped and fell on his back, shattering the two bottles of beer and submerging himself in the pool of who knows what. This really was the absolute low point.

I flew to China to work on some of the elements of starting our own factory—in particular, developing our lasts. I still remember vividly the strange array of meetings from this time: Brendan and I met a guy in a car in an alleyway late at night to pay the bond for our new factory space. Our contact was lounging out the door of his car, cigarette hanging off his lips. I remember visiting supplier after supplier, making excuses for why I wasn't at the factory when our main supplier knew I was in town, using drivers who didn't have a relationship with the main supplier so that they wouldn't be informed of our movements. I saw eye-opening manufacturing, from sophisticated operations all the way through to last makers who still hand-poured hot metal into moulds that were then buried in the ground to cool, with no sense of occupational health and safety in sight.

Meetings at supplier factories were traditionally held around a tea table. They were around the average size and height of a coffee table, only the top of a tea table is a slotted grid with a drain carved between the edge of the slots and the end of the coffee table. The grid was normally made from wood, slippery and dark with tea stains and slimy old tea leaves clinging to the slots—the idea was to pour the tea leaves and liquid at the bottom of your cup through the slots when you finished your tea. The bottom of the tea table was enclosed, normally in a material designed to mimic marble, though not so well as to actually fool the eye. On top of the grid stood an old kettle, matt silver and dented after so much repeated use, surrounded by small ceramic cups. The kettle sat on top of a hot plate plugged into a nearby wall and always seemed to boil in an instant. Once brewed, the equivalent of a shot of tea was drunk. The table almost always held red-and-gold packets of overwhelmingly strong, seemingly unfiltered cigarettes, which were smoked in these tiny rooms. Rolls of toilet paper sat on the tea tables. While at first this seemed out of place (read: I thought it was gross) I eventually came to realise that this was like having a box of tissues sitting on a desk. Totally acceptable and for exactly the same use.

A tea table at a supplier factory

Particularly during this phase I frequently felt an incredible exhaustion caused by a number of factors:

- the inability to communicate on my own

- the need to approach communication from multiple angles to ensure the correct message had been translated

- the stifling, humid heat

- the seemingly circular nature of negotiations

- cultural differences that were so infinite, subtle and daily that I never felt entirely comfortable

- the worry of hitting deadlines and achieving our goals in the face of so many unknowns.

Thanks to Brendan's tireless work and resilience, we did ultimately secure our own factory space. It was a section of a floor of a building. We created storage spaces, a small factory space and proper office space. The floor was painted green, an auspicious colour chosen by our team. We moved our office out of our supplier's building, which afforded us much more freedom and a much more peaceful day-to-day. Then we began to concurrently test other suppliers to diversify our risk. We began to buy machinery, keeping a spirit of 'testing before investing', even in machinery buying. I remember on one visit Michael was confused when he went into our factory space and there was an ice-cream freezer on the factory floor, like the ones you see in service stations or convenience stores. Wondering if it was a cultural initiative, he asked what it was about. But no—it wasn't for ice-cream. It was to test speeding up a cooling process in the making of shoes.

We'd passed a critical barrier in our business. We had saved our supply chain, were on track to diversify it and about to start experimenting with bringing our production all in house by building our very own factory. But while we were putting out fires in China, there would (of course) be a fire on an entirely new front soon.

When competition plays dirty

We had always tracked our competitors daily. Each day when I opened their sites up, I held my breath a little. Would they have done something cooler than we did? Would they have hit the tipping point before us? The anxiety, the race, the emotion was real.

When we'd learned that we had competitors, back in our very early days, we didn't think that they had stolen our idea. To start a company like Shoes of Prey, you needed months to prepare, and they had launched so closely to us that they simply couldn't have seen our site and copied everything so quickly.

So we watched their work closely, with pangs of anguish when they beat us to a great press placement, and we absolutely over-analysed when they did something we hadn't yet. It was difficult to clearly analyse how we were tracking against them when the emotion of competition, particularly in the early stages of the business, feels so personal.

On this particular day in 2011, I didn't even make it to my desk to punch in the URL. Mike had already loaded the sites that morning and was furious. I couldn't believe what he was telling me. I went to my computer and I punched in the URL. The familiar emotional rollercoaster began. I clicked around with anxious concentration, my fingers softly shaking. I opened their configurator (the page where you could design your own shoe) and felt anger burst up from my stomach like lava. I was upset—I was furious—I felt a huge sense of injustice. Their configurator was suddenly exactly the same as ours. Truly, totally, exactly. We had built all of our technology ourselves, and it was leagues ahead of all of our competitors—until today, where one was magically exactly the same as ours. We had sweat, blood and tears in this project. Could they really have figured this out, or had they somehow picked up our code? It just seemed impossible that the site could have been replicated so closely without lifting our code. We were livid. And as you may remember, all three of us co-founders are ex-lawyers.

We strongly considered engaging lawyers. The competitors had previously also lifted our blog posts and reposted the content as their own. If we posted tips for preventing blisters using sticky tape? There it was on their site 24 hours later. We said cobalt blue is trending? They said cobalt blue is trending. The feeling was totally maddening. And I failed to feel the flattery in it.

As we talked it out, someone suggested that maybe the coders our competition had hired had done this without telling them. It was plausible, but still, not comforting. I wanted to be stoic but didn't have the capacity.

We had such clear evidence about what had happened. While we had not registered a patent, the copyright would still be on our side. We spoke with our contacts in intellectual property law. We knew our case would be strong, but we also knew it would be very expensive. I had spent a reasonable amount of time working in litigation when I was a lawyer, and I knew that if we moved forward and it did go to court, it would take a long time and a lot of our attention.

Normally the first step in a litigation case is to try *not* to litigate: a 'cease and desist' letter is sent. Michael, Mike and I drafted a very strongly worded letter and sent it by email. Their response was in the same tone. We then used search engine optimisation to our advantage, and posted on our business blog about what had happened. It ranked more highly for their brand name search than their own website did.

They took their copied configurator down shortly after our post went live and returned to their previous one.

While we got the right outcome, this interaction set a tone that I'm not proud of. I think there is much to be gained by competitors at least having a civil relationship, particularly where there is a market large enough for many players.

If I had this time again, I would not have followed the same steps — I would have picked up the phone first. I would have found a way to be human before resorting to aggressive semi-legal measures.

But this is an insight only gained from hard personal growth, and becoming more stoic in the process. Speaking of hard personal growth …

When fears are confirmed instead of allayed

We caught up late one afternoon. I'd always felt a certain kind of deep, personal anxiety whenever we caught up. However, this person was connected to the business and I couldn't avoid them. And yes, I am being deliberately vague because, while I want to share my experience of this moment and relationship with you, there is no benefit to this story for me to name and shame. I don't know their side of the story; I don't know what was happening in their life that day. I only know what was happening in mine.

I was grappling with depression. My business, just like my personal life, was complicated and unmappable. While I was professionally thriving and part of me was loving the challenges I was facing, I was also under an incredible amount of stress and just getting out of bed every morning was a war. Every morning I had to consciously make the choice to reboot.

We sat in front of one another without any particular agenda. Eventually, as a way of framing some feedback, they said, 'You're just not a natural entrepreneur, and people think you're fake. You should stop being so fake'.

I wasn't listening anymore; I was just hearing that my fears were true. I was so gutted I could barely breathe, and directed my energy to controlling my tear ducts. My worst fears were confirmed. I already had a perpetual voice in my head that told me that I was total rubbish. Now it was being articulated by someone else, openly and directly.

I sat silently and absorbed what I'd just heard. Hoping to turn it into a learning moment, I asked, 'How do I appear fake?'

Imposter Syndrome had taken over control of my thinking and I'd accepted the comment that I wasn't a natural entrepreneur. I'd quickly and silently tallied all the times I'd not understood something immediately, had to look up an acronym that had been casually mentioned in the course of conversation, or done something that hadn't gone as I'd thought it would, and could see why someone would conclude I wasn't a natural entrepreneur. I didn't know then that all these things were in fact normal.

Now, when I look back on that statement, I don't believe it for a second. While I may not have been the kid at school who set up shops and sold lollies in the local neighbourhood, it didn't mean I wasn't entrepreneurial.

But *fake*. That hurt. I gently asked for more information. I didn't even know how to carry myself, suddenly painfully self-conscious in the face of feedback like this. Their response boiled down to something about me showing too much interest in people, and smiling too much. I was so confused.

Confused because I didn't have the confidence to back myself to this person and confused because even in my haze of self-doubt, this just didn't make sense to me.

Constructive feedback, destructive mindset

More than once along the journey of building Shoes of Prey I received feedback that was painful. Sometimes it was incredibly helpful, but other times it wasn't constructive and I should have dismissed it out of hand and continued on. That's hard to figure out in the moment, because there are so many internal emotional responses happening. They can vary from:

- embarrassment: 'I knew it, I do suck at this'.

- defensiveness: 'You're wrong and now let me tell you why you're wrong!'

- anger: 'And just who do you think you are?'

It takes a little time to separate from the initial emotional response. My go-to emotional response was almost always along the lines of saying to myself 'I knew it; I do suck at this'. It was such a natural, quick reflex.

With the clarity that comes with hindsight, I can see that the feedback was vague, not actionable and without any particular objective—it was not feedback, it was just a set of subjective comments. I felt confused, demotivated and wondered if similar conversations were happening throughout the business. There was a good chance they were—we were all young and learning as we went on areas like people management.

We needed to train our people on how to deliver feedback at every level of the company. This only became crystal clear to me when I passed the emotional response I had in the moment. At the time, perhaps the most difficult aspect of being told people thought I was fake and that I wasn't a natural entrepreneur was that they were such deeply rooted personal anxieties. They confirmed fears that I had carried around my whole life, like my head on my shoulders; that I'm not likeable and I'm not capable. That fear had manifested in ongoing anxiety and depression, before I'd even received this feedback. My brain then took any opportunity that proved my self-criticism and piled on, telling me I was just awful at everything.

During this time I was so deep in this mindset that I simply stopped seeing the point of life. There is a vast space between this feeling and taking action on it. I am one of the lucky ones who never crossed over into action, but there are many others who aren't as lucky.

In that time there was no hope. I lost the capacity to feel joyful. I managed myself socially by focusing the conversation on others and I learned that it's easy to keep someone talking about themselves without having them realise it. By doing this I studiously avoided anyone digging too deeply upon asking me 'How are you?'

The only way I can describe my experience of life at this time is like swimming in the dark with no pinprick of light or sound to guide me to anything. I was just completely adrift. This stretched out from days, to weeks into months. A constant numbness had permeated everything. Nothing sparked joy and I held absolutely no hope for anything. And when I heard feedback like this, hit a road bump in my work or anything else that seemed to align with my self-perception at that time, I took a little step further into the bleakness.

I cannot even remember when the true depths of this started. I stubbornly avoided antidepressants. I felt that was for people who couldn't figure things out. It was for people who needed actual medical attention. And I'd heard antidepressants were addictive. The last thing I needed right now was a dependency on medication. I opted for anything and everything else—trying therapy, sleep, exercise, a clean diet and meditation. The only problem being that I couldn't find a therapist I clicked with. The exertion of exercise drove me to tears when the adrenalin rose in my body, and meditating was kind of a joke: my mind used the silence to unleash all of my fears.

I finally decided to talk to my doctor. I really liked my local doctor. She was about my mother's age, and had always offered practical medical advice to try out before writing me a script. 'You have the flu? Have you been resting, drinking lots of fluids? No? Try that. Then if you're still sick in three days I'll write you a script.' I liked her approach and manner. In its own way, having her tell me to rest, in her capacity as a doctor, gave me the permission I needed to take a sick day. I decided to talk to her about what was happening. I prefaced the conversation with 'so I'm not at risk or anything, you don't need to report me' (I had for some reason built up this idea that maybe there was some organisation she'd tell and I'd end up on a watch list somewhere, triggering warnings whenever I applied to do something in future). I went on, 'But I just don't really like life anymore. I haven't and wouldn't do anything but, yeh … um, I just feel really sad all the time'. We talked over how long I'd felt like this and what I'd been doing to try to combat it. And then something really practical happened, which oddly put me at ease. She had me do some short multiple choice tests in which I overperformed (hah). These tests were standardised to determine if you qualified for a reduced fee number of psychologist appointments — which is great, because they're expensive. And, they assisted doctors in standardising whether a patient really did pass the threshold for being put on antidepressants.

When the doctor suggested I start antidepressants right away, and knowing her usual approach, I trusted her. The first week or two I just felt dry-mouthed and tired. Maybe even faintly headachey. And then, six weeks later, for the first time in years I began to feel hope, joy and myself once again. It crossed my mind at this point that maybe I was 'better' and no longer needed to medicate — but upon researching I found that this was a common misconception. Six weeks is about when the antidepressants really start to work, so to stop then would have been a huge mistake.

With the chemicals in my brain playing nicely with each other again, I felt not only the relief of this turning point, but finally space to open up into a new chapter of life.

CHAPTER 14
WORKING WITH YOUR EX

By now Shoes of Prey had its first round of funding, around 20 people in our Sydney headquarters and three years of trade under its belt. I was fully focused on our product aesthetic, brand and public relations. Michael was still far more operationally oriented and considering drumming up interest for a new round of funding.

Michael and I always thought we kept our working relationship separate from our personal relationship. What we didn't appreciate was that our personal relationship dynamic was to carry on until the end of our time working together. The dynamic between us was not malicious or intentional on either of our parts. I by nature was a pleaser, and Michael by nature was a manager. He delegated well and I, as a pleaser, wanted to take on everything he delegated. When I look back at myself, I can see it's connected to my lack of confidence (and my arch nemesis, imposter syndrome, which used busyness as a measure of personal worth) and my desire to be liked. I would inevitably take on too much, feel overwhelmed and not deliver on the insane amount I'd committed to. Michael would rightly be frustrated. And so it would go: we would repeat the cycle with him trying to manage me and me trying to over-please. A recipe for disaster.

This need to please and lack of confidence would manifest in me hitting a type of paralysis, avoiding emails and discussions that felt out of my depth, when really I needed to jump in, have a go and learn along the way. But that's not how it went.

The breakup

Michael and I knew it wasn't working. For 12 months we'd been actively trying to fix it, but with no change. We went to therapy, we meditated, we talked with friends and family, we read books ... we did almost everything you could imagine to remedy our relationship. And eventually, in early September 2012, sitting in our little one-bedroom apartment in Surry Hills, we finally called it: it was over. I felt relieved that there was finally a resolution. I felt afraid of the unknown. Would I be single forever? What would my friends and family think? I was so aware of the fact that we'd never, ever relate to each other the same way again. We'd never wake up beside each other again. We both sat in this sadness, but also rose up. We both insisted that the other take everything (!) so to avoid an impasse we ended up splitting everything as fairly as possible. Happily, we didn't have a dispute over Hunter. One thing we were in complete agreement about, however, was that there was no way this would affect Shoes of Prey. We were both as committed as ever to the company, and what with the growth and potential that lay ahead we couldn't afford to miss a step.

By a stroke of luck another apartment had come up in our building, so I was able to move out within the week. I know it might seem totally odd that we chose to live in the same building, but sometimes small steps are the best to take when there is such a huge issue being dealt with. It also allowed us to come and go from the office in the same direction so that we wouldn't need to tell our team about the separation immediately.

The first two weeks after the separation were incredibly exhausting. I had moved into a new home. I was mentally dealing with the weight of what we had just decided. I was attempting to remain focused and to not let on to anyone in the business about what had just happened. The effort of getting out of bed and forcing myself to reboot every morning was herculean:

> Get up. Don't hit snooze again. Or do. I'm so tired. Eat breakfast. Wait. I don't have a fridge. Or plates. Shower. Find clothes from packed boxes. Buy breakfast on the way to work and force it down, chewing mechanically even if I don't have an appetite.

I was totally exhausted. For the first time in a long time I got to the office around 9.30 am and left at 5 pm every day, eating whatever I could reach and falling into bed as early as possible. Bed had become an Ikea mattress on the floor of an empty apartment; random boxes and items were organised as best possible in a space that had no furniture. I felt very alone — I was 30 years old and I didn't really know anyone who had been through a divorce other than my beautiful friend Aron in London, who supported me as much as he could by sharing his experience, but even with this confidant it all just felt so ... unmappable.

My friends were amazing through this time, but there were moments that they couldn't be with me. And the reason I got through those moments was Hunter. She was a little, purring, furry godsend. In my most vulnerable moments, just before I fell asleep and when I woke up each morning, when I truly felt adrift and alone, this tiny little furball was curled up with me. Coming home to find this loving presence padding around the house was important. Hunter is the only pet I've ever had (beyond goldfish) and in this time I really understood the bond between animals and humans.

It was two months before we told our team or the board that we were separated. In Australia you have to wait for a year of separation before filing to make the divorce official, and you have to be able to prove that you had in fact been separated for that full 12 months. So there was nothing publicly pressing to announce this, since our actual divorce was still a ways off. However, it was only a matter of time before it became obvious — it was becoming challenging to conceal that I'd moved out, and eventually we would both want to start dating. To have our team or board find out about our separation accidentally, or from an outside source, felt like it would be a betrayal of trust. And besides, it felt as though we owed some kind of duty to disclose, particularly to the board members who had invested in us.

We thought through how we were going to tell our team. Should we call them into a meeting room one at a time? No — people might come out looking sad and the rest of the team would either think we were firing everyone, or the person would just tell everyone and we'd lose the chance to properly frame the news.

Eventually we decided to tell everyone in teams. We were still pretty small and close knit, but ultimately there was no attrition. We had already shown them how it would be: for the full two months before we told them, not a single person had even guessed Michael and I had separated.

Of course, this was one of the risk scenarios that our board and shareholders had worried about when they had invested in us. I always felt a cold nervousness wash over me before board meetings, and that day it was more intense than usual. Because we didn't have a meeting room big enough for our board, the bar next door allowed us to hold board meetings in their upstairs space that was empty and closed to the public in the daytime. We trod up the stairs, making small talk with our board members, getting coffee orders taken and settling into the space, which was an odd but awesome marriage of antique French, farmhouse and 1960s interior design permeated with the faint lingering smell of last nights drinks in the carpets and soft furnishings. Looking back, this whole scene is ridiculous. How did we ever have serious meetings in this space? But at the time my mind was so far from how the space looked and smelt. How would they take it? Would they want one of us to leave the company? Would they care at all?

To their credit, they absorbed the news in silence for a moment and then Rick Baker spoke up to ask us the tough questions that felt so awkward to pose, but the board really did need to ask. He asked how we felt about continuing to work together and about any practical impact it would have on the business. When we shared our answer, the tension in the room was palpable. And then ... we moved on to the next agenda item. It went as well as we could have hoped.

I'd like to think that our team and board were so resilient in the face of our news because of the culture we'd built.

How to build culture and why it matters

When we started out, our team was small enough that the cultural values were obvious. There were about eight of us, sitting in close proximity, and we crossed over each others' work significantly. All of this fostered a very organic understanding of what we were doing and why.

When we reached 15 people in our headquarters, in our cool new office with corporate graffiti (so startup), subtle but important changes started to occur. For example, there were disagreements over the tone of our emails — how many exclamation points were too many? Was it appropriate to put a smiley face in an email reply? 'Warm, approachable and customer-centric' meant different things to different people, and the friction was intensified because each person passionately believed that their interpretation was the best way to uphold our company values. Whatever they were.

When it became clear that we'd need to formalise our values and culture, our team shared the company culture document that had been put in place at Netflix. (It was publicly available on Slide Share.) Mike, Michael and I had read it over and spent a Sunday working out what the first draft of our company values would be.

The first thing we realised as we debated each slide of the Netflix culture code was that, to us, it felt like a whole lot of sticks and very few carrots. We suspected that our team didn't really want to sign up to this, but that the clarity of the mission and values was really what they were looking for.

Still, the Netflix culture code was a really great base to start from. We debated each value they had mapped out and tried to imagine functional applications of it. Then we defined what our values were, based on what we thought was a model way to behave in delivering on the Shoes of Prey values, day to day.

The great thing about this was that it not only developed our values, but it flagged a whole lot of process documents that we needed to create. For example, a leave policy, tone and voice guide for our marketing and communications, and standard office hours.

In hindsight, we had been remiss in not defining simple things like these. But we had been deliberately ad hoc because we:

- really enjoyed the flexible nature of the office ourselves

- had all come from corporate environments that had their own strict parameters that felt almost infantilising

- wanted to create a level playing field for parents; in previous workplaces I had seen people who didn't have children resentful of their relatively longer working hours and lack of flexibility, so we thought if we could create a place where everyone had the same flexibility (and responsibility) then this would never, in theory, be an issue

- knew we weren't paying market rate for our staff (which we made up for by giving everyone equity), and so we looked for perks that we could provide that might help bridge that gap; we thought that this flexible approach was one of them.

Throughout the exercise we came to realise that these same motivating factors that underpinned our values could carry on in the cultural architecture. The important difference was that with cultural architecture — our values — we would make sure we were all on the same page in terms of our expectations of one another and the work we were doing from the outset.

After a lot of brainstorming—not only among ourselves, but also with the team—we created our first culture code. I've put the complete document in Appendix A.

Above and beyond the document, we implemented our culture code by adding a culture component to our staff reviews. At that time we also had a 'daily huddle', which comprised of the following topics:

1. *Good news.* A business win, a call-out to say thank you to a team member, or to highlight some great work or a culture code implementation, and celebrations like birthdays and work anniversaries.

2. *Numbers.* How we were tracking to the metrics that we'd isolated and focused on for that period of time.

3. *What I'm working on.* Each person had a maximum of 30 seconds to call out what they'd be focused on that day.

4. *Challenges.* This was an opportunity to solicit help from the team on issues, mention any upcoming leave or to lay down a challenge.

As you can see, we actively sought to call out in the 'good news' section of our daily huddle when we saw our team delivering on the culture code. This also helped to ensure our team had practical examples of how to implement it.

And lastly, as leaders, we led by example wherever we could. After all, any team would only ever hold themselves to the same standards their leadership team did.

Attempting lifestyle changes

My lifestyle had changed significantly by the end of 2012. Not only was I now separated, but we had also decided to capitalise on our early momentum in the United States and engage a US public relations agency. US press had already been receptive to our concept and sales were slowly trending upward without any investment from us. With the scale of the opportunity there in the size of the market alone, these early indicators felt worth exploring. I was constantly meeting, emailing and on the phone with Australian press and building towards something similar in the United States, which meant I needed to travel there with reasonable frequency. I was also travelling to and from China working on our product.

I'd also been building relationships with designers in the United States to do their shoes for their fashion week shows. I had hoped that this would deliver on many objectives that were important for us at this stage of the business and brand. It would:

- position us in the minds of shoe-lovers as a fashion label that belonged in the company of the brands we would work with

- give current customers a reason to buy another pair of shoes from us, and new customers a reason to tip over the edge and buy a pair of shoes

- provide an exciting reason for fashion outlets to write about us.

And on a personal note, I absolutely loved working on these projects. Our shoes were instantly part of a lifestyle and entire look. It really helped people understand how to design and wear our shoes.

With so much travel I'd started to feel like I was in the air more than I was on the ground. And to be honest, this hype, this constant movement and exposure to environments that weren't home, were amazingly fun distractions.

At this stage I still hadn't mastered the balance between being a pleaser and actually getting everything done. I'd agree to do a task and forget about it among everything else. I'd decided not to reply to emails that really needed a reply, believing that email shouldn't be my priority. I didn't manage my communication well. In short, I was a nightmare to work with.

And eventually my team told me. Even they didn't know how to articulate the issues to me clearly. No-one around me shared any direction that was specific enough for me to pick up and work on. In hindsight I needed a coach to work with. But we couldn't afford that. So instead we had months of circular conversations where we kept trying to resolve my working style.

I remember sitting in a Thai restaurant in Surry Hills, knowing that we co-founders were there for feedback to be shared. Over betel leaf parcels and spicy som tum the feedback I got was that I was great, and that I just needed to be focused, prioritise my tasks and get the work done. Of course this feedback was all true, but not specific enough for me to really connect with and action.

Another feedback session occurred 'interrogation style'. It had been suggested that the co-founders have one person sitting in front of the others receiving feedback, before we changed places. This could have worked, except in this instance the emotion that arose for each of us while sitting in that seat was so great that it overshadowed the insights and constructive messages. It also played directly against the fact that none of us were all that comfortable with confrontation. It wasn't really in our culture. (Debate was; confrontation was not.) Eventually we got there, but that process was long and painful. Although I was experiencing this feedback colleague to colleague, it really showed me how important it is as a manager to develop your reports with clear, direct feedback. And that must be followed by a clear, executable, time-bound plan. Otherwise, no-one feels anything but frustration and failure—on repeat. It wouldn't be until much later that we would properly implement feedback training and systems that really worked well. I'll cover more on that in chapter 17.

When I was at home in Sydney (drumroll) I started to take some weekends off. One of my really close friends had expressed concerns about my mental health, and pressed me to at least try to be computer free on weekends. It was hard, and I didn't strictly adhere to it while I was in the process of regaining colleagues' trust by getting done everything I said I would get done. Sometimes the guilt of the pile of tasks waiting for me on Monday was so much that I'd start feel sickeningly anxious about the work I could be doing.

Reboot Hack

To combat weekend anxiety, I'd pick up my computer, start hacking into a task until I really understood the size and shape of it, and then decide if I really needed to get it done on the weekend, or if I could schedule it into my week. It was honestly the only way I could assuage my anxiety around it.

Also I started to log things I thought of in my calendar as tasks to do the following week. This was probably one of the most helpful tricks to help me see that they will get done and I can take the weekend off and actually relax.

Looking for other ways to regain my balance, I also started to allow myself to do 20-minute power naps instead of using caffeine to adjust my body from jet lag when I was on a really intense schedule. I get really nauseated when I am jetlagged, so rather than push through it and drive myself crazy, I found a way to work with it.

Genuine balance wasn't something I ever achieved during the course of Shoes of Prey. Now that I'm on the other side of those years, while I am shocked at the way I lived my life, I'm still not sure that I would have done anything differently. That being said, I am glad that I have redefined my approach to life, because I can see that I was missing some fundamental ingredients for happiness. I always said Shoes of Prey is the love of my life; I didn't really realise at the time that it was.

CHAPTER 15
NEW HORIZONS

It felt that both professionally and personally, the company and I had laid some important foundations. With my newly minted sense of 'normal' inside my head, and the business having overcome some very serious barriers, it was time to step up yet again. The factory team was finally in a culturally sound environment and taking huge steps forward on our own production. There was a larger roster of suppliers to spread our risk, and our sales were growing. I'd found a daily rhythm that felt positive, and even joyful at times. And Michael and I had found a version of how we'd continue working together comfortably.

New partners join the equation

Shortly after our separation, Michael ended up moving out of the apartment building. But he stayed in the same suburb, so we created some (then serious, now funny) rules to try and make the situation as bearable as possible. Here's what they were (well, the ones I remember):

- If either of us got into a serious relationship, we'd make sure we told each other early on so we could deal with any emotions gracefully.

- Surry Hills has a lot of amazing restaurants and is a pretty great place to go on a date. Given we both lived in the area, it felt like it could be a minefield, so we loosely divided the neighbourhood into two areas so that we wouldn't run into each other on dates. He took from Cooper Street out towards Redfern, and I took the other side, from Kippax Street to the city. (No one wants to run into an ex on a date.)

- No dates would meet either of us at the office.

Michael started to date more seriously before I did and, to his word, he told me about Katrine, who is now his wife. As they became more serious it seemed unreasonable for her not to meet him at the office, so that rule was lifted—but I did ask for her not to spend time in the office. No-one could have known at that early stage that they would marry, and the situation was so confronting. I know this wasn't a particularly evolved thing to ask of Michael, but I did. Although we were both totally sure that separating was the right thing for us, seeing a new partner in the office space was emotionally confronting and avoidable. For me it was critical to preserve the working relationship.

This became interesting when I met Vuki. We were looking for a great public relations agency and had decided that whoever was doing the PR for Kogan.com was the agency we wanted to work with. (Kogan.com is an 'Australian portfolio of retail and service businesses' and is regarded similarly in Australia to the way Amazon is in the United States.) After a quick Google search, it turned out that it was the agency that had just moved in across the hallway from our office a couple of weeks earlier. I popped across the hall and knocked on the door, and there was Vuki. We began our professional relationship and, after Shoes of Prey had moved to a new office, we began dating without breaking the rules.

Eventually Katrine and I met. We emailed with one another beforehand and set an open tone that I'm proud to say has permeated our relationship to this very day. And this open tone was critical—we had many direct and clear discussions. I know over the early years we frustrated one another, but I truly believe this was baggage related to the roles we played in one another's lives (ex-wife, new wife) rather than it being a product of either of us personally. I am incredibly grateful that Katrine was so evolved as to be able to work through these moments with me. A rare and incredible gift that I am lucky to have experienced.

It was time for new frontiers both personally and professionally at Shoes of Prey so, naturally, we began to wonder if we should have a physical retail store.

Bricks or clicks?

We continued to ask our customers what they wanted from Shoes of Prey through our social media channels and soliciting more directed responses through the occasional survey. But they couldn't always tell us exactly what they needed, and it took us time to realise that. It might have been because they couldn't articulate it, or that they didn't know they wanted something until they experienced it, or simply that friction points they were experiencing didn't bother them enough to mention. Because of this, we had to not only ask questions, but also watch their behaviour to figure out the insights.

It's like that famous Henry Ford quote (that has never actually been recorded as being said by Henry Ford): 'If I had asked people what they wanted, they would have said *faster horses*'.

A great example of this was a question our potential customers frequently asked us, which was: 'What do these shoes look like in real life?' We had a number of projects to address this question. We:

- built out a 'leathers' page where we posted large-scale, up-close images of swatches of each material available

- offered to send swatches of materials to customers

- posted images of swatch combinations to customers via email, or replied to this question on Facebook

- posted images of as many finished shoes as possible across all of our owned platforms.

But we couldn't help our customer to experience what the shoe felt like on her foot. And this is a big deal when buying a pair of shoes. So, after much debate, we decided to open a physical store.

Of course, we didn't just decide to do it and then go ahead and open a store. There was a lot to consider. Would we open a standalone store, or would we open a store inside of a department store (also known as a concession)? We quickly decided that a concession made the most sense. The shoe floor of a department store already had qualified footfall (which means people walking past already thinking about buying the product) that we didn't have to build and drive alone.

In Australia there are two major department store chains: David Jones and Myer. We needed to not only look at which would be the best fit for our brand and target audience—we also needed to pique the interest of both to ensure we had considered all possible options properly. Michael spearheaded long negotiations that led to this outcome. One of the key factors that played in our favour was that department stores needed to drive footfall. And housing our only offline retail store, with us directing our entire audience to it, would do just that.

For us, it was a very back-to-front journey to go from online to offline. We needed to learn the age-old craft of offline retail, while our predecessors were scrambling to understand the online retail that came much more naturally to us.

The new complexities that this added to our business were vast, including:

- integrating with existing POS systems
- introducing infinite numbers of shoe styles and sizes to a traditional retailer
- training staff to not only sell but design shoes
- creating a returns process; could customers return shoes to the concession? Where would we store them if they did? How would we process them in the systems if they had not been bought through the concession, but instead had been bought online?

But we did solve the minutia ... and it turned out to be something pretty special.

The in-store experience

Our first store opened in Australia in January 2013 in David Jones, in their flagship Elizabeth Street store in Sydney. Our concession was positioned at the top of the escalators when you reached the women's shoe floor. For the design of the concession, we worked in partnership with The General Store, a retail agency that was started by Matt Newell, who had been my catalyst for considering a career change out of law and into advertising. In return, when Matt asked me if he should open his own agency, I pushed him over the edge to do it. It was such a wonderful 'coming of age' for our companies to work together on this project.

Our first store was special. Truly special. The General Store presented us with concepts that would see us collaborate with architects, composers and fragrance houses to make our little corner of the world an experience. The concept was to build a space that was made almost entirely from things we made shoes out of. This truly got to the heart of showing our ability to bring shoe designs to life, and it simultaneously engaged our customers with all of the elements that they would have at their fingertips to build the shoe of their dreams.

The centre table was padded with the same material we used in our shoes and covered in leather. Embedded into the leather were iPads for you to design shoes on. This meant that when you sat at the table and inevitably started to press your elbows into the leather as you leaned towards the iPad to design, you felt the same softness that your feet would feel when you walked in our shoes. And each of the seats was made from a different leather texture.

From the middle of the central table sprouted sculptures made from shoes. They soared almost 2 metres above the table, with shoes forming the leaves of 'shoe flowers'. The shoes had been designed to replicate the shape and colour of the flowers we wanted to emulate. The idea was to draw people in with this bold artwork, and then open their minds up to the possibilities when designing their shoes.

There was a light fragrance of white tea and thyme that permeated the space. Again another sensory cue to stop, slow down and be in this space with us.

Matt was not only incredible when it came to retail creative solutions—he was also a professional musician. So when it came to thinking about how we wanted our store to *sound*, he knew how to approach it and who we could work with. We really had a lot of space to dream. Together we built a soundtrack that traded out traditional instruments for layers of sound: high heels clipping along instead of drums, and recordings of a deep bass purr from my cat, Hunter.

All of these elements did multiple things. They:

- helped people to instantly understand that we were not a regular off-the-shelf shoe label

- created a space that was slower, more engaging, less insane than the bustle of shopping usually was—which was necessary when designing shoes

- gave even more of a reason for foot traffic—the store was a curiosity that people wanted to visit.

We had the option of having the store staffed by the David Jones team, or staffing the store ourselves. In Australia at the time, department store sales staff worked from a salary, without a commission element—so we weren't concerned about how to incentivise them financially to sell our product. However, there was a reasonable amount of specialist knowledge needed to sell our shoes. You had to understand not just good fit, but also the basics of shoe construction and how our technology, systems and processes worked. So we opted to hire and train our own team.

When customers arrived at the store, they could sit at an iPad and, with the assistance of our team, design their shoes. They had access to swatches of every single material available so that they could match colours and textures as they designed on screen. We held our most current silhouettes in stock so that customers could see similar shoes in real life. And we also held our entire size range across key styles so that our shoe-loving customers had the opportunity to try shoes on to make sure they felt comfortable that they had chosen the correct size. Not only did this give our current customers that additional information they wanted, it also opened up an older clientele to us who were less comfortable ordering online.

And it worked.

The store did double its forecasted revenue in the first 12 months, which made it the highest revenue per square foot on the floor against brands such as Christian Louboutin, Jimmy Choo, Steve Madden and more.

The General Store submitted the store to the World Retail Awards. It was announced shortly after that we had become a finalist, up against Karl Lagerfeld's concept store in Paris, and Puma's flagship store in Osaka. It was the most flattering, insane thing to happen—particularly since it was our first store. The awards, which none of us attended, were held in Paris. It felt unreasonably optimistic to fly to Paris for an award that had competition like Karl Lagerfeld. The night of the awards we all went home and to sleep, as usual. In the early hours of the morning, unbeknown to each of us, our phones were lighting up. We awoke to discover that we had in fact won the World Retail Award for the World's Best Store Design 2013. Luckily, representatives from the Australian Retail Association were there and collected the award on our behalf. It felt like a dream—it truly didn't feel real that we could belong in this company on the world stage.

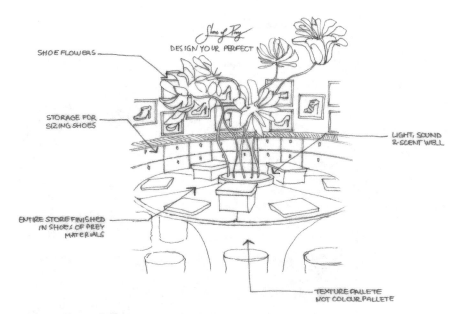

Sculpture by Stukelstone.

Source: The General Store archives

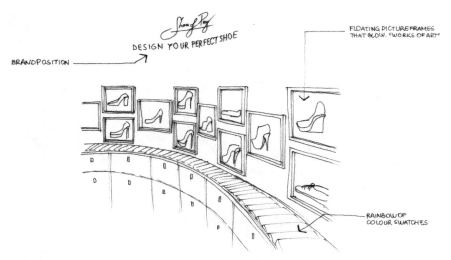

Some design sketches of our David Jones store.

Source: The General Store archives

During the build process at David Jones.

The finished store.

Yet we did. And suddenly, with the recognition and approval of the World Retail Awards, we had credibility that opened doors to CEOs of large retailers who now knew who we were. It rolled out in front of us a network of highly experienced retail mentors. And it would propel us into entirely new spaces. Particularly, into the United States.

Pitching Nordstrom

As I mentioned earlier, I'd started to work on our public relations in the United States, following on from the organic traction we'd already had there. By now we'd completed further rounds of funding and they had largely come out of the United States. Our networks were building and so was our reputation.

We had seen businesses such as Bonobos, an e-commerce menswear company, partner with Nordstrom and grow their businesses enormously with this distribution. Nordstrom is a family-owned department store chain in the United States, famous for its excellent service. And importantly—it started as a shoe retailer, and to this day still prioritises shoes in its retail offering. So we knew that if we were going to enter the US market, we wanted it to be with Nordstrom.

We hunted through our networks until we found a connection to Nordstrom and ended up with an introduction to the head of footwear. We spent months communicating via Skype and email without gaining traction.

We needed a new card to play. So we told a little white lie.

Mike was attending a wedding in Seattle, which is where the Nordstrom headquarters are based. We contacted the head of footwear and said we were all going to be in Seattle shortly (white lie) and would she like to meet?

We landed the meeting and Michael and I booked flights. We spent the entire day before the meeting on the shoe floor of their downtown Seattle store. We spoke to team members and learned their pain points in selling shoes to women. A few themes emerged. Nordstrom:

- used to sell a much larger range of sizes, but no longer did; salespeople often encountered people they could no longer help when they came to the store

- had a styling team that were excited about what this meant for their customers, which also included brides, who seemed very underserviced in the footwear department

- had a strong tradition of 'clienteling', which is building long-term relationships with their customers, taking the time to learn about their tastes and needs to be able to proactively recommend items they might like; our service would mean that they didn't have to wait for new stock of shoes to come in. The staff could simply design and suggest shoes to their customers.

Armed with this information and our pitch, we waited in the meeting room at Nordstrom HQ. After 15 minutes Tacey walked in, and after introductions she let us know she had a hard stop in 45 minutes. We would need to talk faster than expected—our pitch time had just significantly reduced.

We first talked Tacey through the direct applications of Shoes of Prey to Nordstrom, as we'd learned from her staff the day before. Our meeting pushed past 45 minutes into an hour, and Tacey eventually checked her watch, surprised at the time.

Then she asked us to come back the next day.

Within six months of our meeting, we were opening our first concession store with Nordstrom in Bellevue, Seattle. And not long after that, Nordstrom joined our syndicate of investors. The data we had gathered from our first store was incredibly compelling. We, alongside Nordstrom and a new round of investors, decided that expanding our business through stores would be a scalable path to success that was well worth funding.

We agreed with Nordstrom to roll out a total of six stores: San Francisco, Orange County, Chicago, New Jersey, Washington DC and the original in Seattle.

With so much activity in the United States and an organically growing audience there, it seemed that we needed to spend a lot more time in that market. I'd believed we needed to be there for many years, and had even proposed we move the company there years earlier. A move there had seemed inevitable to me, even though we didn't have a map for what that might look like:

- The population size alone made for an exciting opportunity.

- There were much more sophisticated freighting options.

- It has better time zone crossover with our European markets.

- The talent pool was experienced in ways that, in general, we were still learning and developing in Australia.

Each time I had travelled to the United States I'd found an environment of people who were so open to new ideas, experienced in their area and keen to make meaningful introductions for you. And because the market was so much larger and more developed, the introductions were truly amazing. Each time I set foot in New York, I felt like I could make anything happen if I just had my focus right.

I desperately wanted to move to New York and get this show on the road—yesterday.

Phase 6
On Moving and Grounding

Moving our headquarters to the United States and opening stores in Nordstrom would prove to be one of the most memorable experiences of Shoes of Prey. We truly banded together as a team and moved mountains. It would also be the year that I had no fixed address, looking for ways to be emotionally and intellectually grounded before I finally settled into my own space in Santa Monica, California.

CHAPTER 16
A NEW FACTORY IN CHINA, A NEW OFFICE IN AMERICA

Back in China, after Brendan's legwork in researching how to start our own factory, Chris was our new factory manager and Chief Operating Officer. He was the first manager we'd hired who had shoe and factory experience: he'd built and run a men's shoe factory in Taiwan and had a great analytical mind. We'd previously brought him on as a consultant on our supply chain and trusted his strategic view of the world. In fact, he and his wife, Szuting, had come to China with us for a series of meetings when we first began to consider building our own factory. In my opinion, Szuting was Chris's secret weapon. Strikingly intelligent and very wise with people, Szuting was Taiwanese born and fluent in Taiwanese, Mandarin, Cantonese and English. She understood not only the language but also the culture we were working in, how business was done and how shoe manufacturing worked. In meeting after meeting, she was able to listen and watch, understanding nuances beyond the words that were being said. Not only did this help us to negotiate better, but it also helped us to understand our counterparts' behaviour in a way that significantly reduced the friction and emotion of the negotiations.

Chris was tasked with taking our factory from the experimental test kitchen that it had been to a fully fledged operation: the first-ever large-scale, purpose-built on-demand shoe factory. Which, with a little less jargon, means the first factory that was purpose-built to make one pair of shoes at a time, on a large scale.

While this in itself was enough of a challenge, Chris would also face visits from the local mafia and strict and detailed regulations for foreign entities that locals were not often required to comply with. We received frequent advice to throw off our adherence to the rules: it was expensive, operationally complicated and often slow. But we chose to stick by the rules.

Chris also had the task of hiring and retaining staff. We had seen first hand the issues that attrition in factories could cause, and we did not want to spend our time chasing new talent. We needed to recruit talent who would develop with us these totally new systems and processes, then stay with us to execute them. The type of training we'd have to do if we had a high turnover rate would be a huge drain on resources.

While this might seem like a clean corporate gig, it was tough in ways we'd never imagined. For example, we had established a canteen in our factory to make meals for our staff, which is usual practice in China. However, the chefs fell out one day over how much sugar should be in a dish. The fallout was so intense that one chef dumped water into boiling oil, causing hot oil to cover the kitchen and leading the other chef to chase the offender through the kitchen, lunchroom and factory with a meat cleaver. By a stroke of luck, there were only very minor burns suffered. But the point of this story is to say that nothing is simple about people management in China.

Designing the factory

No-one knew how to build an on-demand shoe factory. We consulted with people who had been in shoe manufacturing for a long time, but many just couldn't or wouldn't step outside their incredible expertise in mass manufacturing to consider another model. And it stood to reason: manufacturing is complicated and detail-oriented. Changing just one element would ripple through many systems and processes. Reimagining the entire thing felt to them like a reinvention of the wheel.

And in some ways it was. You may remember me sharing an example in chapter 13 of lasting. I'll recap—very generally speaking, lasting is the process by which the top part of the shoe is attached to the bottom part of the shoe. Mass-production factories frequently spend hours setting the machinery needed for lasting one particular style, and then they just produce that one style all day or even over many days following. Because every single shoe coming down our production line was totally different—for example, it could be a pump, followed by a flat, followed by a sneaker—we had to find new ways to prepare the lasting machinery that took seconds to set up, not hours. Our team worked with the manufacturers of the lasting machinery to develop exactly this.

My team told me a story about this time that I love: a small group was put together to consider the flow and layout of the machinery in this new, on-demand factory concept. They laid out large sheets of paper on the floor and worked to scale as they debated how to get the best efficiencies. They were working through a multitude of issues, from the most efficient arrangement of the factory in terms of the order of processes the shoe must go through, to how to reduce the number of steps any cobbler needed to take in order to receive, make and send on their part of the shoe. In the background another worker continually bothered them. He had ideas on how to do this! But, knowing that all too often too many cooks spoil the broth, the team asked him to wait until they'd done their work.

But wait he would not. Without any tools to express his idea, he built out his idea of a factory layout in an excel spreadsheet. He had even tailored the cell sizes so that the entire proposed layout would be to scale. And it was breathtakingly good.

One of the Shoes of Prey cultural values was to ask for forgiveness, not permission, and this was the moment that told me was that these values had permeated even our China office! In my previous experiences with team members in China, it was difficult to elicit a sense of proactivity and creativity. Yet here it was. Ideas can come from anywhere. And that bias to action? It made me grin from ear to ear.

Playing by the rules

With investors and a business that was rapidly growing, we didn't feel that *not* playing by the rules in China was an option. We were also concerned for the safety of our people on the ground. We'd all read press about executives going to jail in China for participating in dealings that may have made some cultural sense at the time, but fell squarely outside of the rules. And we could see how this could happen. From the early stages of establishing our factory, we had received visits from the 'mafia', and there is even a carjacking on record.

Another challenge with playing by the rules is that rules frequently change. A great example of this was the introduction of environmental licences for factories. It was a multi-stage process, the first step of which was a document that allowed you to go through the process. There was a quota for the number of these documents released in any time period, so we hustled to make sure we got one and then proceeded to work through the remaining stages of the process. However, some of those stages of the process were delayed, because even the government didn't know how those stages worked just yet.

Our dogged compliance did put us at a disadvantage, particularly when compared to well-networked, locally owned and run businesses. We dealt with long, expensive wait times for regulatory approvals while we watched counterparts sail along cleanly without them. It begs the question — should we have just kept working with local suppliers even if, from what we understood, they were operating illegally and unethically? Who knows. It didn't seem possible at the time. It's one of the many unmappable decision points I ponder when I find an idle moment.

Our China team

I always loved visiting our factory—it was a highlight of my Shoes of Prey experience in many ways. While there was truly wonderful stuff happening in our headquarters and other offices, the factory was the place you could smell, touch and see what it meant when someone clicked 'buy' on shoesofprey.com. The printer would churn out the page showing the order details, and shortly after that page would be joined by the materials and start its journey around the factory, producing the shoes that had been ordered somewhere in the world at the click of a button. It was one of the few times that I felt proud, excited and really struck by what we had managed to achieve. It felt like magic.

The team there were truly awesome. Matt Carlon, our head of sourcing, remains, to this day, the most Australian man with whom I have ever crossed paths. His turn of phrase still brings a huge smile to my face when I think back on it: 'bewdy' was his typical mark of approval and words like 'strewth' were never too far from reach. Ruben ran our product design, and had such a passion for the right fit and aesthetic. He had built and run his own shoe factory in Spain, and he truly understood what we were trying to build. He brought that critical bridge of shoe-making expertise and invention together for us. A character, with arms covered in tattoos and a wonderful Spanish accent, Ruben was someone I loved to work with.

Simon was an incredibly kind gentleman with a moral compass that could not be faulted. He ran our factory teams, and it was clear that he held the respect of each and every team member. Monica was a quiet, slight girl, hugely intelligent both in logic and with regards to people. She ran our sourcing, before being promoted to Assistant Manager of Production, a very senior role in manufacturing and one that not too many young women in China rise to. Helen ran our shipping, Forrest our China finances, and Howard oversaw it all. Howard was an unusual find in the realm of industrial China: he understood the approach we had taken to culture and people in our headquarters and was the key to translating this into our China team. A translation we could not have done effectively without him. Of course there were many more. Lily, Shifu — too many to list. They were amazing.

Moving to the USA

With all these things in the works, the headquarters team and I still had the next challenge to tackle: moving operations to the United States. I landed in Seattle in mid November 2014. It was freezing: a bitter type of cold I did not know how to live in. We were preparing to open our first concession store with Nordstrom, within their Bellevue store. It would be a test store that would determine whether we rolled out more stores with Nordstrom in 2015, so the stakes were high. I logged on to Soia & Kyo, a Canadian label, thrilled to finally have a reason to buy one of their winter jackets (but concerned about how quickly they could ship to me). My next action was to email the team about product development. We'd been considering boots for a long time, but hadn't really focused on them. I emailed the team, 'We need to get going on boots! Did you know it's so cold here that you can't even wear ballet flats!?' (Like I said, I was so inexperienced with this kind of cold.)

I was staying in a serviced apartment. On my first night there, still in my pyjamas, I sat on the couch, pulled a blanket up around me and flipped open my laptop. I felt distracted by the silence, so I switched on the television. *Keeping up with the Kardashians* filled the screen. I'd always thought the Kardashian family were expert marketers; sure, I rolled my eyes at some of the antics, but you really cannot help but be impressed by the empire they've built. And, as a girl who loves both beauty and fashion, it did appeal to me from those perspectives. Watching the show I caught that glimpse of a home life I could relate to in some ways — family bickering and the procrastination that preceded almost every workout I did. Less relatable were the cars, mansions, plastic surgeons and so on, but that made it novel to watch. When the ad break started, I was jolted into remembering where I was. Ads for prescription medication were followed by piles of fast food ads, all 'under $5 a meal', and law firms demanded I get what was owed to me by signing on to their class action litigation. It was so American, so based in a different cultural mindset.

Never had it been clearer to me that we needed to be in the US market to be able to understand this customer, who was so different from the Australian woman.

NYC, LA or Seattle?

We debated a long time about where we should land the company. Here's how we thought about each place:

- New York
    - close to fashion and consumer press
    - close to fashion labels for collaboration
    - great talent pool to hire from
    - upcoming startup scene with a focus on fashion tech companies
    - challenging time zone differences with the China factory
    - potential for the city to consume us (if you've spent time in NYC, you'll know what this means!)
    - good base of investors
    - a lot of shoe companies are based on the east coast
- Los Angeles
    - local to celebrity influencers
    - better time zone crossover with China factory
    - 'Silicon beach' was starting to be established
    - close to investors in San Francisco
    - not as much of a culture shock from Sydney for our staff
    - talent not as expensive as they were in San Francisco, but close enough to recruit from there

- Seattle
  - close proximity to Nordstrom headquarters, who we'd be working closely with
  - other large tech companies were already based there, so there was some good infrastructure and capacity to attract talent to this location.

You can probably tell by this checklist that I was significantly biased towards New York. We debated this vigorously, but in the end went with Los Angeles — realistically, issues such as time zone differences were going to be untenable from New York.

We invited our entire Australian headquarters of 24 people to move with us. Our team was reasonably young and without too many adult responsibilities (children, mortgages, etc.). We were all in this really special time and place together, where we had so much freedom and so much opportunity. The business was still growing quickly, the strategies we'd implemented seemed to be working, and we were pushing the boundaries of our business and ourselves as individuals every day. Roles were constantly expanding, with team members stepping up to new responsibilities with determination, engagement and courage. There was nothing to lose. Of 24 staff, 22 said yes.

The move

The reality of moving triggered a huge amount of personal administration that began to hover like heavy clouds over each team member's head. There were so many questions to address. So, rather than have each of 22 individuals do their own research, we created a checklist that covered everything from visas, taxes and healthcare to dining tips in our new neighbourhood. Of course the team still had a huge amount to execute for themselves, but this list meant that the research was done once, for everyone. (See Appendix B for a copy of this checklist. Of course you'll need to check what's still relevant, as it's a little bit old and specific to moving from Australia to the US, but it may be a good starting point.)

We rented a large house in Venice Beach for a few months and it became the place everyone stayed when they first landed and looked for a house of their own. Not everyone could move at the same time, so these staggered arrivals had a soft landing place. It was such an active, warm, exciting environment to be a part of as we started this new chapter of Shoes of Prey. It was like a cosy clubhouse where we often ended up for shared meals and weekend drinks as the sun set. I live in Venice Beach now and frequently drive past it. When I stayed there, I stayed in a very small room annexed onto the rooftop area. It swayed with the breeze, was a bit inconvenient to get to, very pokey and warm, but had the best views in the house. I look at it from my car as I drive past and still feel the warmth and fun of the time we spent there, ready for a big leap into the unknown.

The roadshow

As the Sydney headquarters were moving and settling in, a large chunk of that same team were preparing for what we affectionately dubbed 'the roadshow'. We were scheduled to open five more stores with Nordstrom—this time, all within a 10-week period. This included the store builds, launch events and our first days of trade for each store.

A smaller group of us started 2015 with the 'pre-roadshow', which was a month-long trip that covered each of the five stores to prepare the store managers, their teams and ourselves for the detailed mechanics of the rollout. I also carved out time to meet with our top 10 local customers and influencers in each location. They were our best advocates and became the grassroots champions of our launch in each city.

As I began January 2015 in the United States, I had no fixed address. Everything from my apartment in Sydney had been boxed and was being shipped to a storage space in California. Hunter, my cat, was staying with Vuki in Sydney until I had an address. I strained and broke our relationship this time, as work and the distance were just insurmountable, but he remained in the fibre of who I was. All I had was my suitcase and a hotel room. I didn't know it then, but this would be my reality for the entirety of 2015.

Can you imagine it? Never having a single full-sized bathroom product. Only wearing clothes that don't need to be ironed. Always eating out. Living out of one suitcase. Having no fixed address. Missing important family and friend milestones and weddings, and not being in one place for more than a week. For a full 52 weeks.

Our pre-roadshow team consisted of Brendan, Todd, Lydia and me. Brendan was the very intelligent generalist introduced in chapter 13 and he had moved from his role as factory manager into managing the build and installation for each of the stores. (Dave, Mike's brother, ran the factory before Chris came on board.)

Todd had joined us years earlier in Sydney as a product manager. He would now diversify into the project manager for the stores, and he was the font of knowledge when it came to the United States. He was from Laguna Beach, California, and had the answers to everything we didn't know about his homeland. He is such a responsible, caring human being—who also taught me some of my best travel hacks, such as, if you have a shirt that needs ironing, just put it into a dryer with two ice cubes and you'll get the wrinkles out. Awesome, right? The sum of all this earned him the affectionate nickname 'Dad'.

Lydia had been hired initially in Customer Happiness to work on the David Jones store. She had outstripped every role we'd put her in. She is Scottish and I loved both her accent and approach to life. She had a sense of fun, was very insightful with people and knew the words to almost every song that I heard when I was in her company.

The ten weeks of store launches were up there with some of the most incredible weeks I experienced at Shoes of Prey. Brendan was running the store build outs, and had been working closely with the builders for some months. He worked with them and the Nordstrom team at each location to ensure the smooth installation of our stores. While this took place the rest of the team would be coming in from other locations and preparing the elements they were each responsible for. Engineering would be setting up the iPads and in-store software, Annabelle would be preparing for the launch event, and Anna and I would be meeting with press, influencers and shooting local content. Launch days were hard deadlines, and no hour of the day was off limits when it came to getting things done.

Anna had joined us after leaving a career in law (it became something of an inside joke that we were in the business of rescuing lawyers from law), and a stint teaching English in Korea. Her first task was working almost like an in-house counsel to close our third round of funding (worth US$5.5 million), which was closing during the opening of our Seattle store. Then she worked to set up that store. And then she led our public relations efforts. Never have I seen someone so adept and thorough in each area they engaged with.

Annabelle had joined us from our David Jones store team. She was young, had boundless energy and determination, and an unfailing desire for responsibility and progression in her career.

Joel was also present for most of the roadshow. A kiwi gent with no off button, Joel headed up our marketing. There were three things I loved about working with Joel: his data-driven approach to marketing always included space for gut instinct, he thought broadly about marketing and its role within the overall success of the business, and he had just the right amount of irreverence.

I still remember the night before the launch of our first US store, in Bellevue, Seattle. We were on the Nordstrom shoe floor at 4 am, K-pop was blaring from my iPhone and Chung, one of our talented engineers who had jumped in as part of the 'all hands on deck', was doing snow angels in the debris from unpacking.

Though the days were intense, we always found ways to have fun. We made sure to take at least one day off in each city all together. In New Jersey it was over Easter weekend, so I hosted a big family dinner in my serviced apartment. There was a raucous Easter egg hunt, which I still have footage of. (Let's just say you don't get in Anna's way when there's chocolate to be found.) In Washington DC we did a scavenger hunt around the city that started with building a house of cards (geddit?) and ended with barbeque.

We also had additional people who weren't part of the Shoes of Prey team become part of the family over the course of the roadshow.

Janie Bryant was one of them. Janie was the costume designer for *Mad Men*, which was then airing its final season. We developed a collection of shoes with her that we featured in our stores as they launched, and as part of that Janie joined us for each launch event, truly becoming part of our ragtag team. My favourite moment with Janie was the night of my thirty-third birthday. We were in Washington DC, opening the Pentagon City store. The whole team had congregated in my hotel room. We were noisy, cakes were everywhere alongside a chocolate sculpture of Capitol Hill and there was a giddy atmosphere after long days spent locked together doing demanding work. Suddenly there was a loud knock at the door and, as I started to open it, an even louder voice yelled 'Would y'all keep it down in there?!' The room fell into an instant hush, and I opened the door further with my heart in my throat. Were we about to get thrown out of the hotel?

Nope.

It was Janie, who had just pranked us. Really, really well. She came in and the buzz resumed for a fun, warm evening together.

Natalie and Rowan were others who were adopted into the Shoes of Prey family. While all this was going on, we'd also decided to start the Jodie Fox YouTube channel. It felt like a great way to share what we were building, and the experience of it. We knew our customers were savvy women, and might even appreciate the company behind their beautiful shoes. Rowan and Natalie joined me for part of the roadshow to film and edit a series of videos. Natalie is Natalie Tran, otherwise known as 'Community Channel' on YouTube, a true OG of YouTubers and still one of the funniest people I know. After working through the tasks at hand for the store openings, I would get back to find my hotel room set up with lights, camera and a smiling Natalie and Rowan, ready to film my next YouTube video. The first few weeks of this were particularly gruelling. Take after take of the same content—we were working to find my tone of voice. And I was exhausted. Looking back over footage that ended up on the cutting room floor, I realised I had been unintentionally 'micro napping' with long blinks as I spoke to camera, the large, bright, white halo light beaming directly into my dazed eyes.

While Natalie, Rowan and I were working in challenging circumstances, they became such a highlight of my day. Their lightness, warmth and consideration created a safe place after the pummelling of the day. We went through some crazy adventures together and I absolutely love and still cherish them being in my life to this day even if by us filming together I was in fact being pummeled a little more.

If this schedule and set of projects wasn't enough, it was about to get more intense.

Aubrie Pagano, the founder of Bow & Drape, a custom apparel service, had invited me to speak at SXSW with her that year, which happened to fall the day after a store opening. I said yes, of course. Finishing up the store opening at around 6 pm, I flew to Austin, arriving at my hotel around 1 am, and was ready to go on stage at 11 am that morning. The NIKEiD team attended our speech and I spent quite a bit of time with them. Over the following 24 hours I did interviews and networked my heart out. After that, I went to the airport and flew to Australia, landing at 7 am, to be picked up and taken to the Channel 10 studios to film content for the telco Optus, who was the sponsor of *Shark Tank Australia*. They had invited me to act as a mentor to the *Shark Tank Australia* finalists who had not won, but were participating in a second round with Optus. The filming day was around 12 hours long. My parents flew into Sydney from Lismore to see me. I took them out for dinner that night, not knowing when I'd get to see them next, and then was back on set at 8 am the following morning for another 12-hour shoot day.

Life was insane.

And wonderful.

And insane.

CHAPTER 17
EMOTIONAL INTELLIGENCE GOES A LONG WAY

In managing people or managing yourself (both equally challenging), emotional intelligence was the superpower I found the most impactful. In the workplace it led to smarter interactions and longer tenures. Personally, it gave me the tools to know what I needed to do to reboot on my most challenging days.

An unsustainable pace

In this time I gave up some things that I never should have. The biggest regret I have is not making it to the wedding of my good friend Fi. It still bothers me to this day that I wasn't there for her wedding. I prioritised being at a store launch. A store that's no longer open, for a company that's gone through liquidation.

I still remember that particular launch. We would always start the day of our store opening by joining the full Nordstrom staff 'store huddle', to introduce ourselves and share information about our offering. We'd play games to share this information, and I normally hosted the talk. That day I gave the introduction and, to Michael's surprise, handed it immediately over to him and rushed off. He handled it without flinching. As I had been speaking I'd felt a sweaty heat rise up my back and creep across my skull. I was nauseated like I'd been on a rocking boat for days. I knew I was about to have a panic attack. I made it to the backroom, laid down on the cold cement floor among the shelves of shoes and let it rise and wash over me.

It was the only way I knew at the time to manage these attacks: find a cool place and let them pass.

But even this wasn't enough to jolt me out of the whirlwind of the roadshow, the filming and speaking. For that it took my nonno passing away.

In his early nineties, after a full life and a long period of deterioration, he passed. I flew back to Lismore immediately. It was this strange juxtaposition, to go from travelling to a new major US city every two weeks on a schedule that didn't really include sleep, to returning to the country town of Lismore with my family. Vuki flew in with me from Sydney.

I was responsible for the eulogy and set about calling each family member to ask for their cherished memory of our nonno. We laughed as we remembered him painting his car with dark-green house paint, using a wide brush. He was so proud of the job, and we were all so embarrassed when a policeman asked him, 'Where'd you get your car painted?' We tried to shrink to invisibility in the back seat as he replied proudly that he'd done it himself. After our laughter subsided we fell silent as we realised that nothing like this would ever happen again.

It was also one of the many times I saw how incredible Vuki was as a human being. Not only did he fly to Lismore to be with me while we were in the middle of a broken relationship, but he also did the boldest thing you can imagine. He, a Serbian-born, Australian-raised man, made *my nonna* lasagne. The humour was not lost on her and I will never forget the smile it brought to my whole family that day, among so much sadness. And, to be fair, it was good lasagne.

When I got back to the United States, the intensity didn't drop. Westfield, a major shopping centre developer that started in Australia, was opening a retail lab in San Francisco and invited us to present a storefront for the opening of the space. We rallied a smaller team from the roadshow and did 'just one more'.

Steve Lowy, then CEO of Westfield, was there and I felt like I was in the presence of a rock star. And as it turns out, not only a rock star businessperson, but also a lovely person.

Towards the end of that year I noticed that my body couldn't seem to get enough sleep. I slept marathons of 19 hours in a row and then would comfortably sleep through the following night too. Naturally, it threw out normal eating times and affected my appetite and much more. It was going to take time for me to recover from this burnout.

By August 2015, we'd opened our office in Santa Monica, California, and we tried to settle in once the roadshow closed. There was a huge hangover from the trip, but not in the way you might think. The team didn't know how to work at a less intense pace. And they were all headed for burnout. It took months of management to pull us back into a sustainable pace, which we finally hit, but not without a few sick and mental health leave days along the way.

Imposter syndrome

Even at the height of Shoes of Prey — the growth, the stores, the financing (we were on the cusp of a US$15million financing round) — I felt like an imposter.

Imposter syndrome is something I encountered frequently on the Shoes of Prey journey — even when things were going well. It's crazy that this even exists, but not only is it real — it's sort of normal. The definition of imposter syndrome is 'a collection of feelings of inadequacy that persist even in the face of information that indicates that the opposite is true'.

I always felt a huge sense of fraudulence around Shoes of Prey because I could tell you a thousand things that my co-founders did in the establishing of Shoes of Prey that I believed were more important than what I did. Because I could tell you about all the incredible things our team was capable of … 99.9 per cent of which I was not capable of. You're probably picking up by now that I'm not, and never have been, good at really believing in myself. I always walked around with this hole in my stomach, constantly questioning my capabilities.

The tough thing about imposter syndrome is that it keeps you focused on the negatives, not the comforting things (much less the positives).

Here's a version of how this plays out in my head:

Logic: Wow, you did some amazing things today!

Imposter Syndrome: What are you talking about? Did you see that idea that came up in the meeting? You really should have been the one to think of that. I cannot believe you didn't.

Maybe you shouldn't even be in that meeting.

Logic: Um, no. Can we please look at your list of things you achieved today?

Imposter Syndrome: Yeh I guess. But, you don't want to get complacent. Celebrating good things might make you arrogant or ungrateful. So better not to look at that list, actually. You have to stay sharp, and you need to feel inadequate for that.

Logic: *facepalm*

On not meeting Bill Cunningham

Imposter Syndrome aside, during early 2016 I felt that I was in a reasonably good place with my mental state and, having now spent years on antidepressants, I wondered if it might be a good time to try coming off them. I spoke with my new doctor in the United States and we built out a tapering and transition plan. Happy with the approach, I filled the prescriptions and merrily hopped on a plane to New York. I was doing a press trip with Anna, who led our public relations. We had such an exciting trip ahead of us. The highlight for me was that I'd secured a meeting with Bill Cunningham, the legendary *New York Times* street style photographer. I didn't necessarily have any expectations of the meeting—I was just so excited to meet the man who had been such an important underlying force of fashion for such a long time. We got into New York and, back at the apartment we'd rented, I popped open the medication I'd picked up for tapering. To my shock, instead of two weeks' worth of medication in the bottle, there were only two tablets, which would cover just two days. Trying to contain my panic, I rang the doctor, I spoke to nurses, I spoke to a local emergency department. No-one could get more medication to me while I was out of California.

Three days later, after 24 hours of being off antidepressants entirely, I was sitting in the café at the bottom of the *New York Times* building, on my laptop working. It was two hours until my meeting with Bill Cunningham. Without warning, I looked down and noticed heavy tears dropping into my soup and over my laptop. I realised I was crying—tears were streaming down my face—and a powerful nausea swept over me. A sharp, strobe-like pain hit the inside of my skull. Anna, seated beside me, asked, 'What's wrong?'

'I don't know,' I choked out. I quickly started Googling and found that I matched all the symptoms of withdrawal syndrome for the antidepressant I'd been on. I turned the screen to Anna and said, 'I think this is what's happening. I have to get back to the apartment'. I was falling apart fast and wasn't even sure I'd make it up the stairs of the village apartment we were staying in, so I called and cancelled my meeting with Bill. I was disappointed, but I would be back in town again soon and hoped we could meet then.

That week in New York I had multiple public appearances — a keynote speech at a *Marie Claire* event, editorial meetings and more. In between events, I stayed curled up in the apartment with the curtains closed until the last minute before having to heave myself out the door and plaster an energetic expression on my face. At the end of the week we finally got to the plane and I hid my face as tears streamed down for the entire five-hour journey. Anna was a trooper, making sure I had what I needed, speaking softly with me and not drawing attention. We landed around midnight and I went straight to the 24-hour chemist to pick up my script, relieved that this hell was finally over.

Bill Cunningham died two weeks later, and the industry lost a true legend.

Years later I have finally found a therapist I love and a psychiatrist who works with both my therapist and me to ensure my medication is correct. I kept up exercising, which I now really enjoy, and find that, while committing to a twice-daily 20-minute meditation still has its challenges, it's something that really does add so much to my capacity. Depression is different for everyone. For me it was a chemical imbalance in my brain. It's not a personality flaw, it's not a weakness. It's not a defining aspect of my identity. It's like having a cold—you just catch it from time to time, treat it and get better.

I know that's a lot to share, and in many ways it's just the tip of the iceberg. But I also know that any time I've been candid about depression, it's been met with relief—to know that it's not abnormal, to know that you aren't alone if you've experienced this too. It's my hope that maybe you'll read something I've shared that gives you that relief, or, if you're lucky enough not to experience this, perhaps it'll give you more insight into mental illness that others experience.

Having reached this place of being able to detach my personal identity from my depression, and being able to manage my depression, my resilience has increased. Previously I spent my reserves of resilience just making it through the day. Today I have a wealth of resilience that has given me the power to go through situations others could not, with my feet on the ground, my stomach strong and my heart courageous.

Of course there are still days I feel like a fraud. But that feeling no longer becomes a dark rabbit hole.

Recognising your achievements

Today one of the tools that I use to stop myself when I am headed down the rabbit hole is a spreadsheet that Vuki suggested to me. It's a catalogue of achievements. Every day I try to write one line in there of something good that happened. It's incontrovertible evidence for an unreasonable mind to calm down, and see that actually, I'm not that bad after all.

Finding home

On 6 January 2016 I moved into a one-bedroom apartment in Santa Monica, California.

I pulled my suitcase behind me for what I hoped would be the last time for at least, say, two weeks. That suitcase had been the closest thing I'd had to a home over the past year. On the way to the apartment I stopped at my new local liquor store and picked up a bottle of Hibiki whisky. Something to mark the milestone. (And, something that I didn't have to finish within a day or a week.) I opened the door and flipped the light switch. Nothing happened. I dragged my suitcase inside, closed the heavy wooden door behind me and went to the kitchen to try the stove and another light switch. No electricity. No gas. I thought I'd had this sorted out, but evidently not.

I know at this stage I could have made life super simple and just gone to a hotel. But this was my first night in my *home.* The first time I *had* a home in 365 days. I didn't care that it would be uncomfortable; I wanted to be *home.* Without power, I couldn't pump up the air mattress I'd borrowed. Luckily the hot water was set up. I pulled a candle out of my suitcase

(I always travelled with a scented candle — it helped me to create a homey atmosphere when I was moving around so much), lit it, had a shower and ordered some food in. I pulled stuff out of my suitcase and spread out on the floor anything that would make sleeping comfortable. Then I pulled out my phone and organised the gas, electricity and internet.

I woke up at 8 am to hear the beep of the fridge switching on and lights turning on: the electricity was connected. In the light of day I looked at my home. Empty, but home. It was in a faithfully restored Spanish-style building from the early 1900s. There were only six apartments in the building. Aside from it being one of the most beautiful buildings I had ever seen, the landlord had carefully picked each tenant — and they were the most amazing women. I felt lucky to have landed into a warm little community of my own. Every single day that I got home and closed my door to the world, I truly felt like I had stepped into a cosseting, comforting and peaceful space that could be anywhere — it was an oasis that felt like a calm European piazza had somehow descended into LA. It didn't feel like anywhere but *home*. After a year of no fixed address, I cherished having a space that was truly mine, where I could totally unfold and unpack both physically and emotionally.

People really are the best

While I was excited about my new community at my apartment building, the community at Shoes of Prey was still going from strength to strength. We had always treated our culture code as a living, breathing entity that would evolve with us as we matured. Alongside this document we developed policies — though they were normally developed as needed, rather than in advance. An example of this was introducing our maternity leave policy when one of our team members fell pregnant and asked what our maternity policy was. This worked well enough for a period of time, but when we surpassed 50 people, moved to the United States, grew into over 100 people and had some status as a company, we were no longer a scrappy startup. People needed us to step up our game so that the administrative side of being employed with us was smooth, rather than distracting from the job.

After moving to the United States and settling into being in the office more, Anna Henderson joined the company under the title of Office Manager/Human Resources. During her time at the company, she was another incredible chameleon, just like Anna Le who I mentioned earlier.

Her intelligence ran far beyond her area of expertise and we were so lucky to have her on our team.

Anna implemented systems and processes for our people, nurtured much better communication across the headquarters and developed all of us into better managers—which is no small feat, particularly when you are working with founders of a business. While I can and will list off some of the things she implemented that helped us with talent acquisition, talent retention and culture, the greatest thing she did was help us to find verified insights into how our staff were feeling and what they needed to feel valued and perform more strongly.

Employee Engagement Survey (EES)

This was a long survey carried out once a year in its full form. It gave us the key themes we needed to focus on and set the benchmark.

Some examples of themes we dealt with at headquarters included ensuring people felt they had the opportunity to reach their full potential. We delivered on this by implementing much clearer and more consistent development goal structures for individuals, and ensuring that their managers were equipped to help them reach these goals. Another was helping the team to feel empowered to switch off outside of working hours by implementing a Shoes of Prey communication guide. Themes differed depending on the office, which made a huge amount of sense given both the cultural and work discipline differences.

The results of the survey were then reported to the executive team who, on digestion, reflected the findings Projects would be implemented to ensure we resolved the issues that had been raised. These were then regularly reported on. Committing to and delivering on an action plan like this was in itself a clear demonstration of our culture and fostered trust between leadership and staff.

We then did three shorter check-in versions of the EES through a third-party service throughout the year, which were used to measure progress, or to identify any changes in course that we needed to make.

Lunch and learn training sessions

This may seem somewhat basic, but providing simple frameworks for things such as 'how to give feedback' can dramatically improve the working environment. In some ways, it just aligns everyone's expectations about how situations will be dealt with, and removes the friction of misunderstanding. Additionally, this helped us to live out our cultural values around this specific point.

Frequent one-on-one coffee catch-ups

Anna Henderson did frequent one-on-one coffee catch-ups with our team. While she never did divulge the details of the catch-ups, she was able to discern in real time insights into what was motivating to our team—or demotivating—so that we could adjust and improve quickly.

The level of trust that Anna fostered with the team created an environment where we could really hear the feedback we needed and act on it. It removed the fear of confrontation that can exist when you have to provide honest feedback to a senior person in a company. In my experience, in that situation, people simply choose not to provide the feedback.

Career ladders

When we started the business, we didn't calibrate the career ladders across the company particularly well. The ladders were developed by discipline, and had inconsistencies in terms of rank (the manager in one part of the business may not be as senior as a manager in another part of the business, for example). Anna developed career tracks that cross-referenced both discipline and the company, which gave our team a clear sense of their stages of progression and removed the potential for subjective discussions between report and manager over next steps.

We ran similar formats of all of her initiatives in our other offices, in which we saw metrics such as high retention that suggested we were headed in the right direction.

However well we executed on culture and people management, there would always be other factors that affected our people. As we grew these factors increased and became open to public scrutiny.

Phase 7
On Failing and Resilience

We are told that failing is simply part of the journey. That, in the words of John C Maxwell, 'sometimes you win, and sometimes you learn'. And while that is true, it takes a huge amount of resilience to make it through those moments with the wherewithal to move forward in a constructive way. Particularly when those failures are public.

Chapter 18
Testing and pivoting

The foundations were laid for our next period of growth. Our factory was working well; our team was doing well; our sales were growing steadily. The US concession stores had just opened. The initial data and testing for our concessions was positive. We and our investors were so excited. All that was left to do was execute on the plan.

When tests fail

You may remember in chapter 12 I spoke about fundraising. One item I relegated to the appendix, but deserves mention here to set the scene for this chapter, is the very top line formula that underpins raising large amounts of capital:

- you want to build a behemoth
- you can acquire a customer for much less than their lifetime value (lifetime value is the number you get when you count how many times the customer repeat purchases from you after you acquired them)
- you have a great team with a solid plan on how to do this

then you might be able to raise money to build a big business.

We of course still wanted to build a behemoth. And we had both a great team and solid plan to do it. We had hypothesised that the physical stores — the concessions — would have a very high acquisition rate (people buying shoes, at a rate that's worth more than what we were spending on marketing and COGS) because:

- Our research told us that 'seeing shoes in real life', alongside the factors listed in chapter 12, would provide the tipping point for many of our mass-market customers.

- Being on the shoe floor of department stores put us in the middle of our target audience while they were in the mindset to buy shoes.

- The credibility and halo effect of having a physical space with trusted retailers had reportedly boosted sales for other brands we'd studied, such as Bonobos.

And, our physical stores did have great acquisition rates. But now we needed to scale them.

Our David Jones store continued to turn out fantastic numbers. But whether this success could be scaled was questionable; it was in the David Jones flagship store, which had the highest foot traffic and sales of all their stores. As we examined the prospect of rolling out Shoes of Prey into other David Jones stores around the country, we knew the numbers couldn't compete with what we'd achieved with our first store. In fact, in many cases we weren't sure if we could get them to profitability.

We decided to instead trial opening a standalone store within a Westfield shopping mall in a suburb of Sydney called Bondi Junction. The deal we'd negotiated with David Jones allowed for this and, given our question around scalability, we had to try it. The mall was huge and a very popular shopping destination. As it was a test, we opted to build out a kiosk store rather than open a regular store.

As a side note, I actually think it turned out to be our most beautiful store. While Westfield had some parameters for us to stay within, they were far less onerous than the parameters within a department store. The walls were adorned with artfully placed textiles, leather and the occasional well-placed shoe. It was both surprising and delightful to look at the space and constantly see new details.

But the numbers didn't show the results we needed in order to continue to invest in it. The sales rates weren't as high as we'd projected based on the data we'd collected, extrapolated into targets and were testing against. And the resources we'd need to drive or own foot traffic were significant. After a reasonably short test period, we decided to close it.

In our Nordstrom stores there was an equally challenging set of issues to navigate. In the United States, sales staff were traditionally remunerated with a base salary plus commission. The base was quite low, and the commission was the true motivating factor that I believe is responsible for making retail such an exciting and viable career option in the US market.

In stores like Nordstrom, where salespeople were selling both custom and off-the-shelf shoes, it was difficult to incentivise them to sell a shoe that took time to be designed, instead of quickly selling something off the shelf. The economics didn't make sense for sales staff. We tried many different commission structures, yet in doing this, we hit other friction points. While we needed to balance out the challenges of selling our shoes relative to those on the shelves, Nordstrom had many other brands' needs to balance too. It would not be a good look if it appeared that we were incentivising staff to sell our shoes over those of other brands.

Return shoes were also an issue. Normally returns would simply be resold, but in our case it was difficult because the shoes had been custom made. And Nordstrom had a returns policy that was even more generous than ours. While the policy itself is drafted very openly, there are tales (whether they are true or not), that give an indication of its generosity, such as the story of Nordstrom accepting the return of tyres that they had not stocked for decades and had been used by the customer for 20-plus years. This meant the return rate in our Nordstrom stores was much higher than anywhere else in our business. Our return shoes were sent to Nordstrom Rack, their chain of outlet stores, however the sale of these shoes was still challenging given the unique nature of each item.

These issues were not boding well. But, there was an even bigger issue at hand—despite our compelling customer research and delivery on what we had learned from this data, we had not cracked the mass-market by going offline. Our value proposition wasn't resonating. This meant that it wasn't tenable to invest in expanding our network of stores with Nordstrom, no matter how much sense it seemed to make on the surface. We had taken a conservative approach by only opening a small number of stores and monitoring them very closely. With the data we'd acquired from this test, we found that the stores would not be the scaling point for our business. We needed to reassign the resources we were investing in the stores. When I say 'reassign resources', I will be clear and honest—a part of that was making redundancies. We closed all of the stores across Nordstrom. We also closed the store in David Jones Sydney as, although it was profitable, it was not scalable.

It's never fun when a test doesn't work, particularly one that required a lot of investment. Investment in this case had been monetary, company focus, our personal energy and belief in this path. It had also been a huge amount of human capital—a whole team of people had spent months on the road in a new country to set everything up. And the stores team had continued to spend months on the road, training and supporting our new stores. On top of all this, the closure of the stores, although the right move, was a very public failure of a test. It invited scrutiny that just made it feel all the more awful.

Shortly after this, our co-founder Mike left the company. Mike was at his happiest in our days of taking huge risks with very little to lose. His strategic capacity, engineering skill and fearless execution were an asset at any stage of a business, but his heart was happiest in the much earlier stages. These discussions spanned over many months and, when it was finally time to tell our team, my heart was in my throat. I'd planned to be a 'strong leader' for the team at this announcement, but I couldn't hold in all the emotions. It had been challenging working through having a co-founder leave the business. There were many uncomfortable complexities in the details of how to build out a role and hire to cover the work, how to deal with shares held in the company and, most importantly, how to share this news with the team without demotivating them.

We carefully worked out the messaging, and announced it to the team late one weekday afternoon. It was a shock, but the team seemed to understand. Mike invited conversation and answered questions over the following days as he prepared to finish up in the office. Although we were a young team, there was a high level of emotional intelligence.

As it turned out we didn't lose a single person as a result of the news.

The financials leak

I was hyper aware of the impact that consecutive failures or pieces of bad news can have on team and stakeholder morale. In quick succession we'd had our stores close and a co-founder leave. Yet these things come in threes.

Our finances were leaked on two occasions. The first was perhaps the most painful. I received a call from Kasi at our public relations agency, Sling & Stone. (Full disclosure: Vuki is the founder of this agency and, yes, I removed myself entirely from the selection and appointment of a PR agency to avoid any conflict of interest.) She told me she'd had a call from a journalist who was able to reel off a significant amount of our data to her, proving that he had in fact received our financials. I asked her to send on any email correspondence she'd had from the journalist and when I opened the email, I read with disbelief. I could feel my heart rate and adrenalin picking up. I had held out a little skerrick of hope that this was a bogus claim from the journalist. But. There was our last month of financials.

Hands shaking, I called Michael to let him know what had happened and realised about two minutes into the call that this was scaring him too. I decided to take control of the situation. I told him not to worry and not to answer any press enquires about it. I asked for him to be available so we could catch up later—I would need his help to pull together all the information I needed to build my response.

We'd had a much higher spend (commonly referred to as 'burn') month than usual, which we had planned, and we'd just closed all of our stores. While we would have preferred otherwise, we'd tested the store concept responsibly and it hadn't been successful. But a narrow view of the data, just an isolated month, wouldn't demonstrate this. We were also not willing to share any more data than what had already been leaked, so without context, a catchy headline would be easy 'Shoes of Prey overspends and looses revenue'.

We usually shared some financial details with the press, but never in detail. In high-growth, high-risk startups there are constant fluctuations. We kept our shareholders up to date, but managing public perception of these constant fluctuations was a recipe for huge distraction that would not add to the business, so we generally did not participate in it.

The situation with the journalist was compounded by the fact that in two days' time I was due to speak on a panel at an investor summit—I was to be the first on stage, at 9 am, in front of thousands of people who had backed the fund, and had, by virtue of that, invested in Shoes of Prey. The timing was not ideal.

I emailed the journalist and he sent back a set of questions. I prepared all the answers and then went back over the financials he'd received with a fine-tooth comb to make sure I had not missed a single number. At the beginning of my reply I wrote, 'As a private company we don't usually comment on our financials or on speculation about them, but seeing as you have obtained this information, we'd prefer to help you understand what they mean.'

I kept our conversation on email. This needed such precise handling that I couldn't risk a phone call where tone or off the cuff conversational comments might play a role. I walked through the financials with him, line by line. I explained anomalies, such as the drop to zero revenue in our Nordstrom stores—this was the result of us having closed the six trial stores. Information we had already shared publicly.

At midnight the night before my panel at 9 am, the journalist published his article. I was with the event hosts and some of the other panelists.

We'd had dinner and drinks together and were wrapping up the evening as the article came out. We all pulled out our phones and read it in silence.

I couldn't believe my eyes. It had been a waste of time to provide him with answers and walk him through our numbers. His opening sentence was, 'If Shoes of Prey, the Los Angeles-based online retail poster child continues to burn through cash at its present rate, it could be broke next year'. Based on our cash plan, this was a very long bow to draw. He followed on to note that we'd had a fall in cash receipts in our Nordstrom stores 'from $44 677 to just $452 between September and October', but what wasn't mentioned was that we had closed all of our stores on 24 October 2016 so of course the numbers had dropped. We had already announced this to press.

I called Michael, who was in the United States and in the middle of his work day. We talked through the article and matched each assertion with the actual numbers and facts. It didn't take too long—we'd prepared so much information for the journalist that we had everything off the top of our heads at this point. I hopped into bed at about 3 am, knowing that whatever questions came during my panel, I had an answer. I just needed to get rid of the anger in my blood so that I could provide those answers calmly and rationally. Without ripping the journalist a new one, ideally.

The next morning, I received a call from the hosts of the event before I'd left the hotel—they wondered whether it might be better to avoid the topic of the article on the panel. I turned it over in my mind as I walked to the venue.

I walked into the green room before the speech wearing a fiery orange-red lipstick called Lady Danger by MAC. It felt good—it felt like war paint. Sitting in the room was the panel moderator, Alan Kohler, a leading financial commentator in Australia whom I truly respected. And I could see that he had the article up on his laptop screen. I looked at him, smiled and said, 'Hi Alan, I'm Jodie Fox. I respect that you're a financial commentator, and it would be remiss of you not to ask me about what was published today. So please, ask all the questions you want up there. I'll be ready to answer'.

And he did. The first question off the rank for the day was, 'Jodie, tell us about the article that's been published this morning'.

I was totally calm. I'd prepared myself in detail, the same way I had all those years ago before going to lobby at Parliament House. I addressed each assertion that had been made with data. I had no expectation of the other panelists; it was a messy media situation, and I didn't want anyone else to feel they needed to risk being involved. Yet they did, offering additional commentary. One panelist pointed out that startup investments are high risk and often fluctuate greatly in short periods of time, but generally they sit within a broader strategy that anticipates and plans for those fluctuations. I was sitting beside Andre Eikmeier from Vinomofo on the panel and he pointed out that private companies don't have financial reporting obligations like public companies do and that this wasn't something I was attempting to hide behind. I felt strong and supported. And exceedingly grateful.

After the panel, I went to man our trade fair stand. (The fund had asked us to prepare a stand and be available in it to talk to their investors.) For the next four hours I spoke non-stop to a stream of people, answering all their questions and listening to their concerns that had arisen from the article.

Dealing with media

There were many learnings from that day, but these were perhaps the most important:

- You can't beat the truth. Being honest and transparent was literally the best thing I could have done.

- Really think about what story the journalist wants to tell. In hindsight, my perception is that the article was an attempt to short one of the funds who had invested in us. Someone shorting the fund (which was publicly traded), was able to use our strong profile to damage the reputation of the fund by leaking contextless information. We were collateral damage. We figured out who the leak might have been after they leaked our finances again at a later date. Once we dropped them off financially sensitive communications that we weren't legally obliged to share with them, that type of information didn't get leaked again. (More on the second leak in chapter 19.)

- Great journalists want the true story; they aren't out to get you. When you understand the role you each play by virtue of your work, then you can be direct, honest and respectful with each other, as Alan was with me and almost all other journalists were throughout the life of Shoes of Prey.

- Consider what makes for a clickable headline and try to weave that into your chat with the journalist. If you don't, they or their editor will come up with one, and it might not be the angle you're hoping for.

Changing tack: B2B

With the closure of the shops we were once again a 'pure-play'—meaning only online—and needed to find that scalable channel elsewhere. We went back to surveying our customer, analysing the data we'd collected in our years of operation and looking at market data again. We began to test a number of other areas. We explored influencer marketing once again, and concurrently we began to look at offering our services to other businesses. We were hoping to help solve some huge issues that retailers have.

Firstly, if a retailer wants to develop their own product, the process is long and arduous. A brief is given, materials shared, prototypes built and approved at various stages—and normally these are being sent all over the world because the factories are rarely located in the same place as the retailer. And then, once approved, it's graded out over all the sizes needed. Then, finally, it goes into production. The development can take around three months, and then the production can take another two to three months on top of that.

Conversely, if retailers *don't* want to develop their own product, the timeline starts at the stage of needing to find and purchase stock, eight to twelve months ahead of when it will be in store. The problem is, there is very little to indicate what will be trending eight to twelve months later, when the stock does finally arrive. Normally the only information a buyer has on hand is:

- what season they are buying for
- historical data on purchase patterns in previous years
- marketing campaigns they can use to support the product they're buying
- trend prediction services.

But beyond that it's gazing into a crystal ball. Maybe summer will arrive late and people won't be buying sandals as early as they did last year. Maybe there's a random breakout of popularity in fluoro pink that you couldn't have foreseen eight months ago, so you didn't order any.

Or, on the other hand, maybe you ordered exactly the right item, but not enough and you sell out. You could have sold more and made more profit, if only you'd had that crystal ball to know you should have ordered more. You can try to re-order it, of course. However, factories normally need a large minimum order quantity and will take months to deliver it. By then, your customers may not want the item anymore and you're stuck with a tonne of stock.

Retailers also never want to hold too much stock. Stock sitting in a storeroom, not being sold, is not a good investment. But this is really difficult to manage within these parameters.

We had built our entire business to allow product design to happen on our website in a matter of minutes, to be able to order a minimum of one pair of shoes, and to be able to have those shoes or subsequent orders with you in under two weeks.

This meant retailers could order product from us two weeks out from when they wanted it on the shelves, not eight to twelve months out. And they could test a number of different styles, only ordering more stock when they had an indication of what was selling well and what was not.

While the initial cost of stock was higher with us, ordering with us had the following benefits. It:

- almost totally eliminated the guesswork of buying
- significantly reduced the amount of stock held
- significantly reduced the lag time between ordering and having the stock in store
- allowed the retailer to protect itself and its brand from having to discount unsold stock at the end of a season.

It felt like a no-brainer.

We first tested the concept with Nordstrom online. They wanted to be the one-stop-shop for fashion for their customers. But, like all retailers, they couldn't stock absolutely all the styles and sizes of shoes that they would like to — until they worked with us. We worked with their buyers to develop a range of shoes. We built photo-realistic renders of the designs and added them to their inventory. The shoes were available in a huge range of sizes and they were marked clearly that once ordered, it would take just under two weeks to arrive to the customer. A completely inventory-less model.

We launched in the middle of the night midweek, and we didn't do a single thing to promote it. Within eight days, we'd added a full percentage point to their shoe revenue run rate for the year.

It felt very, very promising.

We would now look to add more clients to this model. Some understood it instantly and ordered with us, season after season. But recruiting clients wasn't easy based on our higher initial wholesale cost and brand, which was still growing. On our end, since the margins were entirely different in wholesale, the volume we'd need to do to truly make this business work was staggering. And, if we weren't really careful, we might start thinking about our business model in the same way that mass-production factories did, chasing paper-thin margins, large orders and taking months to deliver. We had to create this new business model.

In 2017, alongside the development of this new B2B business model, our direct-to-consumer business was also starting to explore a new target message: fit. SATRA, a research and technology centre, had measured 20 000 women's feet and compared their measurements to the size those women reported they wore. They found that 76 per cent of the female population should be wearing a different sized shoe, and the majority of these size adjustments meant that they should be wearing a narrow or wide shoe and don't, because mass-produced shoe brands can't stock them due to the high inventory costs. The challenge is that most of these women don't know they're wearing the wrong shoe size, so it's a big education problem coupled with a complex manufacturing business. We also knew that there were many women who were smaller (below a size 6) or larger (above a size 10.5) than the sizes most shoemakers made. In addition to this, there were multiple brands gaining traction around the sizing message. But they were mostly in apparel — no-one was doing this in shoes, despite it clearly being a big issue. It felt like an opportunity worth exploring.

However, our exploration on both fronts was taking too long and the runway was becoming too short. (Runway simply means how much money you have left in the bank to keep the business running.)

We had always been very transparent with our headquarters staff about our numbers. Each week we would sit down as a team and review everything from sales numbers to cash left in the bank and, if projected on current trends, how much time we had left to make our next major step up in profit, or new round of funding.

Cost-cutting that you really don't want to do

As we fluctuated downward in cash in the bank, with our newer growth strategies not gaining traction as quickly as we'd hoped, redundancies became unavoidable. I felt sick. I felt the weight of responsibility. My brain careened off into useless self-flagellation over the smallest things that might have made the difference. We'd had 22 of the 24 headquarters staff in Australia relocate to the United States with us three years earlier. Letting them go meant their lives, their visas — everything was about to change. They'd given so much to us and, although they knew the risks, it didn't seem fair that the story should go this way for them.

We worked through all the preparations for the redundancies, which would more than halve our headquarters team. And we did as much as we could to honour the relationships we'd built and the dedication people had given us.

We thoroughly researched the visa issues they would face and had an immigration lawyer prepare a basic advice note and all the blank template forms that each person would need to address if they wished to stay in the United States.

We provided redundancy severance payouts, even though we were not obliged to in the United States. We obviously had a fine line to walk here, so that investors would not baulk at the money we were spending on severance, but also providing a financial buffer to the people who were being made redundant.

We would offer to sit with each of them to help them figure out what they might want to do next, to provide a reference letter and introduce them to companies they wanted to work for where we had relationships, and offer a resource to help with resumé and cover letter preparation.

Honouring those relationships also meant building a detailed plan for how we would communicate this news with the team, which we worked through with great attention:

1. We reviewed the entire team's calendars to find a time when everyone would be available. We also checked for who was on leave (if anyone) and made a plan for contacting them.

2. Michael and I prepared how we would tell the team and practised saying it to one another. We knew that on the day we

would be very emotional, and having something prepared would help us to provide our message and be a support for people who were going to be having a much worse day than us because of this news.

3. We prepared to dial in to our teams abroad to talk them through the redundancies after they had been made. We did not want anyone in the company to receive this news second-hand—that felt like a recipe for misunderstanding, worry and friction.

4. We were prepared to lose the remainder of the day's work. We would tell the team to spend time digesting the news, packing up their desks (we also offered to pack up for them and ship personal belongings to their home if they were not feeling able to pack themselves), and, for those staying on to spend time with the people who had been made redundant and needed their support. We knew there were a lot of strong friendships on the team and we did not want to stand in the way of the support they would provide.

A few days before we were planning to make the announcement, the team had all decided to go to a local place for lunch. As we were walking to the door I noticed Michael was still at his computer. I went over and gently tapped him on the shoulder. In a low voice I said, 'This is the last time we're going to get to do this'. And so we went to lunch all together, my heart heavy in my chest. I felt like we were skating through the last happy moments with these people who were like family.

Finally the day came. I gathered together the people who would be staying and asked them to come into a meeting room with me. Everyone else went into a meeting room with Michael and our head of HR, Anna Henderson, whose thorough preparation work had allowed us to go through this day so professionally and compassionately. I really felt for Michael; his conversation was going to be awful. Mine would not be easy either, but his was going to be much worse. We had decided he would announce the redundancies purely because he held the role of CEO, and it came with the territory.

It was an unusual group of people I had pulled into my meeting room, so antennas went up immediately. I could see the team looking sideways at one another. I didn't spend any time dressing up the situation; I told them immediately that they were staying on with the company, but anyone not in that room was being made redundant. I explained why, which didn't take long because we had been so transparent with our strategy and financial position. And I opened the floor for questions, of which there were many. 'When will the others leave?' 'What will happen to their visas?' 'Will we do all the same projects, but with less people?' I gave totally honest answers. This was not a time to complicate things.

When the two meeting rooms opened, there were tears and hugs, and we gathered in a circle. Michael and I both spoke and apologised that we were in this situation. It was the hardest speech I have ever given.

That afternoon the team opened some wine and sat together. We talked about the things we'd loved and lived together. One of the team suggested we go around the circle and tell each other what had inspired us about one another. I wondered if it was the shock that was creating this openness; it felt like we were reeling together in our last united moment.

As this was happening in the US headquarters, redundancies were also happening in Australia, China and Manila (where we had a Customer Happiness team and some other administrative functions). I would spend the following days dialling into these offices with Michael to gauge how the teams were going. It was so confronting for everyone. Every night I went back to my apartment totally conflicted. I wanted to call the team members who'd been made redundant. I wanted to do what I could to see them through. But it wasn't appropriate: I was one of the people who had just made them redundant. In this conundrum I spent evenings trying to distract myself with more work. I called my close girlfriends and they patiently picked up the phone every single time to listen.

A week later a LinkedIn message popped up from someone I didn't know. The person writing to me told me that we'd never met, but that afternoon he had been at a restaurant a block from Shoes of Prey HQ, where we had just made our redundancies. He said he'd been seated near two women who were having a glass of champagne together, talking about the company they'd just been made redundant from in an entirely positive nature. He leaned over to confess his eavesdropping and asked which company it was, and then messaged me to say that whatever the culture was that we'd built, however we had handled the situation, I should know that it had been done well.

I couldn't believe it. The rush of relief that came from that message was indescribable; it was one of the best acts of kindness a stranger could have given at that moment.

This was one of the hardest reboots the business had been through yet. But it was just the beginning.

PHASE 8
ON CLOSING AND ACCEPTANCE

During the last months of Shoes of Prey I became the acting CEO and COO, on top of being the Creative Director. And I gave absolutely every ounce of energy, every shred of thought, every moment of every day to what would be the very last push.

It was a demanding 180-degree swing that flicked from zero to 180 many times over the course of a day. I went from striving with everything I had, both mentally and physically, to clear these high hurdles, all the way to smashing into the hurdles rather than clearing them, then falling, getting back up and finding some form of acceptance fast so that I could prepare to face the next hurdle.

Chapter 19
The start of
the real hustle

With the redundancies complete, our runway became a little longer. But we had to implement a plan to secure the company beyond the end of our runway. We hired Ohana & Co., an investment bank out of New York, to work with us on raising a new round of funding. Although the raise was ultimately unsuccessful, Laurent and Kara truly were incredible to work with. And the lessons I learned in the process of working with them are priceless.

Laurent is a French New Yorker with a legal background, experience in starting and running his own businesses, a formidable and fast eye for diagnosing companies, an enviable global network and an elegant ability to hustle to make deals happen. He focused on web tech and consumer and had been very successful. (For the record, if you're reading this and thinking it would be a great movie, Laurent would like George Clooney to play him.) (Yes, that's meant to make you laugh.) Sometimes painfully direct, yet thoughtful and never rude, Laurent was someone I loved working with.

We worked with Laurent and Kara to build our pitch and find our targets for it. In doing so he became so immersed in our business that he often became my first phone call when I wanted to bounce an idea or scenario off someone.

As I mentioned in chapter 18, we were attempting to pivot from a 'design your own shoes' concept to two adjacent areas that leveraged our unique on-demand manufacturing capability:

1. serving customers who have small, large, wide and narrow feet (whether they knew it or not just yet)

2. providing short, fast run manufacturing for other retailers and brands. Shoe factories in China generally require minimum

orders of 1000-plus pairs per style and three-to-five-month lead times for production and delivery. We were able to produce efficiently with minimums of a single pair and delivery times under two weeks.

These two areas were the basis of our pitches. We spoke to funds, companies who would benefit from purchasing us (usually referred to as 'strategics'), high-net-worth individuals and more, across the globe. I spent time pitching on the ground throughout both the United States and China. (I was spending increasing amounts of time in Hong Kong and China, as there were some big opportunities coming to light in terms of both investment and expanding our retail.) The pitching was not only for funding or buyout, but also business development—we were working on building our pipeline of clients for these two areas that were to be the future of the business.

Our runway kept shrinking. Our hypotheses were not paying off quickly enough to demonstrate that we were in fact onto a concept that warranted further investment. We were failing to find that market fit, despite all of the very positive indicators we had seen in our testing. We received a bridge round of funding from our investor group and, when that didn't look like it would stretch far enough, there came a period of time in which we were receiving fund releases on a week-by-week basis. There is almost nothing more emotionally and intellectually challenging than managing a business in this context. Until it got more challenging.

At this stage, our COO, Chris, who had built our most recent factory in China, left the business. And not too much longer after that, Michael resigned from the business. Both would continue to support the business for a period of time, being available to me as I needed access to their institutional knowledge, and Michael would keep his board role.

The hardest goodbye

Michael had left the day-to-day business and, with his wife, Katrine, who was pregnant with their second child, decided to move to her home town in Denmark for a few months. Vuki and I went along to their farewell party in Venice Beach. As the party wound down and I stood in for photographs with the old Shoes of Prey team members, it felt surreal.

We parted ways with hugs and well wishes, and Vuki drove me over to the Shoes of Prey office to collect a few things before I made my way back over to China that week. (We had gotten back together and were having a long distance relationship between Sydney and Los Angeles.) I looked around the room and began to cry.

Vuki wrapped me in a huge hug and told me he understood that it must have been difficult to see an ex, with his family, moving on. I pulled back and looked at Vuki's face, grateful yet again for this man who had such capacity for compassion, to be able to say this without a shadow of jealousy or doubt.

But that wasn't it.

Michael and I had been through a lot together. We had met the week before my twenty-first birthday, married, started a business, divorced close to my thirty-first birthday and worked together every day until I was just past 36 years old. He had gone from being a boyfriend to husband to co-founder to ex-husband to brother-figure. And, on reflection, he had been the person I had seen the most in my life for the past 15 years. In that moment, that constant of my life finally came to an end.

People have often told me how insanely weird they found it that Michael and I had continued to work together post divorce. But the truth is that we both loved the company and didn't feel either needed to leave it. In hindsight I can identify the reasons that was not a great decision, but I can also see many reasons that it was a good decision.

It wasn't great because we had a really challenging pleaser–delegator dynamic in our married life that carried over into our professional world. You can see how this combination doesn't work together, but it was just a product of human patterns and interactions, not due to any malice or ill will. Another not ideal side effect was that Mike and Michael, who had been best friends for a very long time, naturally gravitated even more closely to one another through our divorce, meaning that many times I missed out on conversations about the business that would occur between them in their natural course of hanging out. Again this wasn't malicious; it just was.

But continuing to work together was also a great idea because we'd been through so much that we could be very open with one another about almost anything. We had treated one another with so much respect that we navigated our divorce amicably. Knowing this, we had a huge amount of trust in one another, and time and time again proved this out in the choices we made in the business that would affect both of us.

Regardless of all this, that day was the end of a huge chapter of my life.

Kidnapping insurance

I suddenly found myself as the acting CEO, COO, and Creative Director of Shoes of Prey at the direst of moments in the business. One of our old board members, Kevin, emailed me and said, 'There's always another move...' he left off the remainder of the quote and offered me his support and time to work through this new situation. Kevin was an entrepreneur himself and had always given us clear feedback and a lot of personal resources. Although the email was short, it was something that gave me hope and strength in a dark moment.

From a personal perspective, I woke each morning to a feeling of fear, sadness and upset but I was so focused on survival that I had no time to dwell and give in, so I clawed my way out of it.

I pushed it aside by listening to 'Shake it out' by Florence + the Machine over and over again. It became my warrior song that somehow took all the energy I was giving to fear and channelled it over to focus and strength. It prepared me to ride into battle each morning as I went in to work. I know, I know. It's a cheesy metaphor, but somehow that imagery really helped me at the time. I feel like I owe Florence a personal thank-you for kicking me out of my fear every day during that period of time. That song was my daily reboot.

With Chris leaving the business I needed to get across the running of the factory. As I prepared to make yet another trip to China, I was on a video conference call whipping through a preparation checklist with my China team when one item tripped me up: kidnapping insurance.

What?

The team explained to me that the factory workers had noticed a number of changes we had made. Changes that indicate a slowdown are very quick and easy to identify in a factory: for example, instead of ordering leather to last us for months at a time, we'd started ordering a month at a time. We had also terminated some roles in the factory office. Both of these indicators had set off alarm bells for the factory workers.

In the Chinese manufacturing landscape it was unfortunately common for indicators like these to occur, and for the factory workers to turn up to work one day to find the doors locked, the factory closed and the owner having run away with any remaining funds. While the payment of severance is legally required when you make a factory employee in China redundant, this illegal practice was so common that literally every one of our remaining 140 staff had personally experienced this happen.

As a result of this, when a factory showed signs of trouble a practice had emerged of having the local mafia kidnap the factory owner and hold them hostage for the amount of severance owed to the employees (plus a fee for themselves).

So I bought kidnapping insurance.

The team also warned me that local security guards were likely to be paid off by the mafia, so I needed to find reliable security. I didn't really know how to go about this, so I was just incredibly careful. I had a driver whom I had worked with for years, and made sure I was with people at all times. (Well, except for when I got home to sleep.)

Chris was still with us at the time, and had devised a plan to help allay the concerns of the factory workers. Every day at 4 pm, the factory workers would send in nominees from each team to sit with our China head of finance, who would open our bank accounts and show them the account where we had put aside the severance money, in case of a shutdown.

When I got to China I felt vulnerable and nervous. I didn't know anyone who'd been in this situation before, though I was absolutely certain that I wasn't the first. Not only was this an unmappable moment, but this time I also had no-one's experience to draw on. Even with all this running in the background, I was focused on everything I needed to do and learn while I was there.

Crisis management[1]

I'd landed into China, kidnapping insurance in place. I'd travelled to China a lot over the course of Shoes of Prey, but this time it had been more than a year since I'd set foot into Dongguan. The hotel I stayed in was new and looked as cool as any new LA boutique hotel, with modern design and

---

[1] Our head of sourcing, Matt, had joked with me about calling this chapter 'The turd in the punchbowl', which was a strongly colloquial statement that was once made to explain to a client that we had one small issue with the prototype we'd made them. I still cry tears of laughter when I think of that sentence.

airy space. The hotel was booked under another name, just to make it a little more difficult to find me should the kidnapping situation get real.

My first day in the office I was in a glass meeting room, on the top floor of the factory in China, the standing air conditioner blasting away in the corner. I could see that Howard, the general manager, wasn't himself. He seemed erratic. His usual reasoned, smiling demeanour had totally evaporated. What I was asking of this team—to run through these challenging times with me, keep the people calm and focused and manage our factory operation on the ground—was more than I had ever imagined I'd have to ask.

I was spending my entire day in one-to-one meetings with the management team members and Howard was the first. His head hit his hands and it seemed as though his forehead could be entirely rubbed away by the end of the meeting. He explained to me the daily grind of uncertainty. As our China general manager he was not only managing the challenges of our new approach to cash flow, but also the resulting people issues. Finally Howard made it clear that he and his family were in real danger. He had been receiving death threats against himself, his wife, his son and the beautiful twin girls he'd been showing me photos of just minutes before. Because Howard was the general manager of the factory, he faced similar pressures to ensure that our factory team were treated properly should we close. Only the style of threat he received was much worse than my potential for being kidnapped. I felt sobered and shocked and resolved to protect Howard in any way I could. We had worked well together before, but this awful experience firmly drew us together to fight our way through this, back to back.

I did about five more one-to-one meetings that day. They ranged from Simon, our head of production, standing firmly with me, giving me the sense of a general—a safe set of hands who knew his army and how they would form and fight—to Helen, confiding in me about becoming a single mum since I'd seen her last.

Finally, my last meeting of the day was Monica. I trusted Monica implicitly. She was street smart and book smart, quick to learn and honest. All day, each team member had opened up to me and exceeded the hour I had allocated to each catch up—but Monica was closed. Quiet, giving me one-word answers. I wrapped the meeting in the face of uncomfortable silence after just 12 minutes. I felt totally unresolved and unsure of the future with Monica with so little discussion in the meeting.

I finally walked out of the meeting room, and not long after got into the car waiting to take me back to Dongcheng with Chris. He asked how I was feeling, knowing the emotional depletion from the meetings I had that day. I relayed the heaviness of it, the views that had been shared with me, and we both sat in the reality of the situation ahead.

We had made some redundancies in the factory, and there was a farewell dinner while I was there. We were moving to a skeleton team until we had secured new funding and/or struck our scalable path of revenue. The dinner was at a local teppanyaki place. I'd been looking forward to time with my team outside the factory but had braced myself for the inevitable pain of knowing this was the end of an era. That numbers on a spreadsheet had meant all of these people were now out of a job.

I took a deep breath and walked in. We were seated upstairs, and as I shuffled in with everyone to find a seat I caught the eye of James, one of my first five employees, who had been one of the unlucky lines on the spreadsheet. I had been resilient, honest and strong throughout this awful process. But in that moment I felt it like a punch to the stomach. James had been there from our ridiculous early ideas. He had seen almost every single evolution of our business and worked with us to bring it to life. He had always had an incredible nature. He didn't speak English and I didn't speak Mandarin, but over these years we had not only worked hard together, but shared personal history. I'd seen photos of his family as they grew up, watched as James got a little grey around the temples, and had shared many a meal together with him and the team. The connection was palpable and as I looked at him that night I felt like I had lost.

Tears stung into my eyes and I went to the bathroom—a damp, wet-floored squat toilet. I stood over the hand basin throwing cold water over my face to push the hot tears away. There were hours of this dinner yet to go.

Dealing with hostile buyers

We were well into running a dual-track process Ohana & Co.: we were trying to either raise money or sell our business. We were in the thick of meetings with potential investors and potential buyers. Meeting after meeting felt like beating after beating. The indicators in the meeting would be so positive, yet the commitments that followed were never close to the way we'd left the discussion. After this had happened a few times, and I'd felt my fury rise, I learned to treat buyers with a much greater level of caution.

We'd had multiple emails with the management of a shoe label that was interested in some of our assets. We set up a meeting, and a heavy-set man sat in our boardroom talking over what he might be interested in. My gut sent red flags up, but I kept pushing on with the meeting, thinking perhaps the red flags were just my pride acting up at being in this position.

Eventually, we did a walk-through of the factory, and the man asked to photograph the machinery. I wanted to say no, because there was so much IP in the environment, but I felt it would be unreasonable to say no. To my surprise he turned his camera *not* to the machinery but to the systems and processes on our walls and started snapping. I reacted (and to this day I cannot remember exactly what I said), and his response was to the effect of, 'Oh, I can see how hard this is for you — having to sell all this when it didn't work out'.

My blood boiled and my face burned. That condescension was too far. Yes, I was in a bad situation, but it was now clear that he'd pursued the meeting in bad faith; he was not there to buy the machinery. I felt a flurry of rage, embarrassment and shock.

Unfortunately, it would only be the first time I would experience this. But eventually I found my way of handling it.

We had one of the largest shoe retailers in Hong Kong request to come to our factory for a tour. I was enormously suspicious, because they'd spent our entire first meeting explaining that their capabilities were far superior to ours. No agenda for the meeting was supplied, despite my gentle requests for one. I was still so furious from the previous days' meetings, so I was not in a great frame of mind.

The meeting began with laborious token gestures of exchanging backgrounds and them providing a brand briefing before finally confessing they were looking to do made-to-order. This conversation was stretched to its limits until I finally said to them, 'Would you like to see the factory?' They looked very relieved and followed me to the door, mobile phones in hand.

I turned around and blocked the door. 'I'm sorry, you won't be able to bring your phones. You've not signed an NDA.' They both stuttered and started to argue. I stood in the doorway, blocking the space and holding the handle of the door closed while I waited for their response. I would either open the door and show them the factory, or show them the way out. I held my ground. Finally they turned and put their phones on the boardroom table, and I whipped them around the factory.

Just because our situation was on a timeline, it didn't mean that I should allow our IP to be treated with any less care than usual. And it was absolutely okay for me to stand up for what I felt to be right.

Managing local teams in times of crisis

When I got back to the United States we continued on with our business, this time with a much smaller team. We moved our US headquarters to a more modest office space and changed to our planned course of business to reduce our budgets. But we still needed to do more. Staff was one of our biggest costs, yet we had reduced to an extremely lean team of around ten and did not feel we could or should reduce further. We also were not comfortable with asking our team to defer their salaries while continuing working for us. So in working over the conundrum with the board, up floated the idea of asking the team to work reduced hours.

We had always shared financials with the team, but this was different. I called the team together and gave them a very clear view of our financial position, our runway, and what we were doing to bring new capital in. I explained that we didn't want to ask them to work without pay, and that we didn't want to let anyone else go. Acknowledging that they all had varying financial responsibilities that they had committed to based on their current income (one had just bought a home and everyone, of course, has bills to pay). From there, I asked the team to tell me how many days a week they would like to work if they were to reduce hours and what days they would be. Everyone came to the table and reduced their hours. Based on this, we then built a plan for the tasks that could be done in this reduced time period, and how they would be executed. Handover between team members working on different days would be critical.

I too cut down on my number of days, but ended up still working full time. As a co-founder, I took my reduced salary but felt the responsibility to put the extra hours in. It felt fair, as I held stock that had the potential to be more valuable than some lost salary if we pulled this off. And as a director I did not feel comfortable drawing a full salary at a time where cash flow was so challenged in the business. Plus, I did not want to ask my staff to do anything that I wouldn't do.

As we came within months of the end of the runway (which continued to fluctuate with the ever-changing funding situation) we had a leadership choice to make—was it better to be optimistic, vague or realistic in sharing where we were at with our staff?

By this stage of the business, I was acting CEO, COO and Creative Director and the decision rested solely on my shoulders. Here is what I thought through:

- We had hired a very intelligent group of people. With the level of transparency we had with them, doing anything other than telling the truth would likely break trust at a moment that we most needed it.

- The office was not just a group of employees. They were people who spent time together outside of work. They were people who, time and time again, had gone above and beyond the call of duty with and for us. They had rent and bills to pay. If we did in fact have to let go of anyone, it would be unlikely that we'd be able to give any redundancy payouts, so the next best thing we could do was give them a chance to create options for themselves in a worst-case scenario.

- I knew it was crunch time and we really needed the team to buckle down with us. In the scenario we faced, we'd be making some unusual and fast decisions as the unpredictable scenario unfolded. If the team didn't know why we were doing what we were doing, this leadership style would likely unnerve them, demotivate them and risk them ultimately not executing on things that truly could be make or break.

I decided to build a timeline, in a presentation document that I shared with the team, of the coming months and mark on it the deadlines for all the options we were pursuing. All the way to 'D day': closing the company. This was always shifting based on small amounts of funding that were continually injected, sales and many other factors. I didn't try to hide any information from them. I gave weekly updates (biweekly when things were moving really fast) to make sure we all had the same information, and had open question time at the end of each update.

When we got down to around two months of runway, I told the team that I understood that they needed to be financially independent. That I understood the fear and concern that came alongside the possibility of redundancy. I could see that they were all working with agility and dedication, but also a large cloud looming over their heads. I gave the entire group my blessing to look for other jobs and an assurance of a recommendation from me, on the condition that:

- it did not affect the timing and delivery of their tasks
- they did not disclose our current company scenario
- any activity that fell within work time was carried out discreetly.

Not a single person left. I never once saw someone taking an interview call or dressed up to duck out to an interview. This transparency, bringing the team in confidence and facing head-on into the issue had led us together to exactly the right place.

Managing shareholders in times of crisis

There are a multitude of emotions each stakeholder can very rightly experience in the process of watching their investment gain or lose value. While sophisticated investors know that, statistically, there is a large chance that a startup investment won't work out, there is a possibility that one will offer a high reward to offset and outstrip all the rest.

In the case of Shoes of Prey, we had a majority of really excellent experienced shareholders. They were sophisticated and in many cases had been entrepreneurs themselves, so they truly and insightfully understood the startup machine. However, we did have two kinds of challenging shareholders—one who regularly leaked our finances to the press and another who had very specific ideas about how we should be operating, despite being totally disconnected from our day-to-day strategy and business.

The financials leak (again)

Throughout this confronting journey we had kept our shareholders updated at regular intervals. Admittedly, some of these communications were too raw and should have been much more crafted before hitting send. And we paid for that lack of polish when, yet again, sensitive emails were leaked to the press.

The leak didn't necessarily change anything. One of our investors had a business that was undergoing a very public shorting (meaning there were bets in the stock market that their business's stock would diminish in value, rather than rise), so it did build into that storm. And it created a sense of public judgement upon what was already a very challenging and confronting situation.

Perhaps the greatest challenge was personal. How, in this moment that we most needed to rally together, could one of our shareholders *who were supposed to be on our team* be adding to this pressure by leaking emails to press?

Shareholder friction

One of the greatest challenges for me was not the suggestions shareholders provided to us, nor the questions that shareholders asked. It was when a shareholder without a lot of day-to-day understanding of the business was aggressively pressing opinions and perceptions, accompanied by long lists of detailed questions. And the shareholder copied every other shareholder into these communications.

The challenge here was twofold, because it's very easy to understand where that shareholder was coming from. They had a vested interest in the business being successful. And they had given something meaningful to the business to earn the shares they held. To want to understand what was happening and be helpful in guiding the company to success was extremely natural.

On the other side of the fence, businesses, particularly startups, move at a very fast pace and fluctuate. And on top of that, our business was very complex — spanning technology, manufacturing and retail. The suggestions the shareholder was making were interesting but not relevant to the business today. Our board members, who each had a very detailed view of the business, each worked to reason with the shareholder, to no avail. They were spending time that we really needed focused elsewhere to make the business a success. It was also emotionally draining; the tone of the communications was so off-putting that my perception is that it closed some opportunities for us to pursue critical follow-on funding from current investors who were on this email chain.

When I reverse roles and stand in that shareholder's shoes, I can see myself wanting to press the company and be helpful. But I also truly think that the outcome may have been much better had the suggestions and questions not been so aggressive. Shareholders—their role and behaviour—can be challenging, and not something that can be controlled. A few of the things I did to adjust the behaviour were:

- ending all emails to shareholders with a request for them to contact me directly with any questions or concerns
- contacting the shareholder sparking these issues and asking them not to email the full shareholder group, explaining why this was damaging to the business at that moment in time.

Communicating with shareholders

Here are the things I learned from this experience:

- Be clear and calm with shareholders about the information rights they hold.
- Be gentle and respectful when declining a shareholder request.
- Only ever write emails you'd be happy to see reprinted on the front page of a newspaper.
- Take a moment to really think over what the shareholder is asking. Make sure that, if you decide to decline their request, it is for very solid reasons that you can truly stand by and know to the best of your knowledge to be correct.
- Always respect that the shareholder is in this with you, and gave something to help you get to where you are today.
- Ultimately you have to make the final decision. Be firm, be strong. If you want to get an outside perspective, pick up the phone to other shareholders to see if the feeling is the same among your shareholder group.

Protecting customers in times of crisis

Customers sign up to your idea by making a purchase, and ultimately they are the reason you are successful. They pay for goods and services with the fair expectation that they will, in fact, receive those goods and services.

When a business is in a challenging situation, often they attempt to make more sales to overcome the issue, not fewer. The only way to make the sales in good faith is to ensure that you can refund those sales if you cannot fulfill them, which we did. The customers we had to deal with slightly differently were those with valid gift certificates; it was a much longer process, and I'm not proud to say that in some territories they could not be refunded. Although the number of people in this situation was small, this is something I consider to be a personal failure that I do wish I could change.

Managing yourself in times of crisis

It was about 3.30 pm on a Friday afternoon and I was back in China, in transit from our factory in China to Hong Kong with Chris, our outgoing COO. I'd set up meetings there, and after that in Beijing. We figured this was the best time to depart the factory. It was the end of the day, so it was unlikely that any dramas would ensue and it was a time that would dodge the worst of the border traffic.

About 20 minutes into the three-hour trip, Chris's phone rang. He laughed disbelievingly as he spoke on the phone, but spoke calmly, asking a few questions. He hung up and looked at me and laughed again. Sometimes things just felt so unbelievable. He explained that he'd just learned that after we'd left the factory, one of our office team had argued with one of her colleagues and had to be physically restrained. And, money was missing from our accounts. A lot of money.

In this moment I laughed. I couldn't have imagined or even suspected these issues. They were so far out of left field and so pressingly urgent that it felt equally concerning and comical. I'd also reached a point of thinking, 'Wow. You just can't make this stuff up'. Having the perspective to be able to laugh at the absurdity of the mounting issues in that moment diffused the energy that was otherwise directly heading toward anxiety. It instead went to focus.

A past employee had filed a health claim against our China company. It was very murky, and appeared that the issue had likely arisen while she was at a previous company, but that company had closed and so we were her only chance to make a claim. The case was entered into the legal process and the Chinese government, which is connected to both the courts and the banks, had frozen the maximum amount of money that she would be eligible to receive if the case were to be awarded to her. That amount was US$175 000. Time was ticking down until the representatives from each of the factory worker teams were coming in to see the accounts to ensure that their severance was still there, and this amount of money missing would not look good.

We had to quickly put aside the shock that this money had been frozen, and think about how we would explain this without the situation exploding. It was not lost on me that it didn't look great that money was missing as I had left the factory to go to Hong Kong. We had Howard and our China financial controller Forrest call the representatives in early, and I cannot remember clearly but I think Chris and I dialled in. We proactively opened the accounts and showed them the frozen line. We told them what had happened and, to our relief, they understood. Unfortunately, the understanding came from the fact that events like this were all too common, as a result of the far-reaching government power and linking of functions like banking and the court system in China.

Aside from having the ability to diffuse my worry with laughter, I retained my sense of perspective and calm in this situation by leaning on the relationships around me.

I was in very frequent contact with our board and Laurent. The professional support they gave me in this time of totally unmappable moments was critical for me to be able to continue taking action, day by day.

Vuki and my close circle of friends provided me with the kind of love and support that gave me the sense that I had a safety net of people who would love me regardless of these outcomes. It was a safety net that would never break. This gave me an incredible baseline of strength to reboot every morning.

In these moments I realised that one of my highest values in life and living well was having a true community. Because no matter what age you are or what you're going through, it takes a village to get to the other side.

In one of these board chats I pressed Kevin for the remainder of his quote, 'There's always another move ...'.

It turned out it's: 'until you're dead'.

CHAPTER 20
KNOWING IT'S THE END

The period of time in which we were funded week to week was gruelling and largely a blur. I will never forget the board meeting in which four of the women in the room, including myself, put forward personal funds to bridge a two-day gap the company was facing. Off the back of that I flew to New York to make one last pitch to keep the life support on just a little longer while I furiously fought and hustled to close deals in the background. Deals that ultimately never came through.

Most days ended with exasperation, frustration and not being able to tear myself away from my computer or phone—working, hustling, working, thinking, to just make this come together. But it didn't.

Throughout what turned out to be the last eight months of the business, the board and I constantly asked ourselves, 'Is this the end?' From a financial perspective we constantly measured our runway. From a business development perspective I spent every last second having any and all conversations to make sure we'd exploited every opportunity for fundraising or revenue—even the tenuous ones. Arguably I shouldn't have spent time on all those conversations, but I know that I couldn't end it without knowing I'd really tried everything. (That's not necessarily a good trait, but I know it's part of why I can sleep well at night now.)

I spent significant portions of my time working through each stakeholder's viewpoint and researching thoroughly to understand not only what we needed to do for this process, but also the order in which we needed to execute everything. I ran the order through my head again, mentally checking the details over to keep my emotions at bay.

Ceasing trade

It was 27 August 2018, months after running this loop, day after day. Finally, today was the day I did have to let everyone go. I felt sick. I cried in the car on my way to the factory and, although I really wanted to throw up, I focused my energy into the actions I needed to do. I thought of the quote that is often attributed to Winston Churchill, although he was never actually recorded saying it: 'If you're going through hell, keep going'.

In the two days beforehand, Howard, Forrest and I had prepared all of the termination paperwork, cheques and filings. We met at the factory early that morning. We had a team of security guards, lawyers and accountants who would be there shortly and, once the working day had begun, we would talk with the management team first and then call the 140 people together to give them the news.

But before this day began in the factory, before everyone got in, I picked up the phone.

I called my Customer Happiness team in Manila and gave them the news. They had a four-week notice period from that day, so I would have time to work through things with them. I had them pull a report of all the people who had bought shoes and wouldn't receive them, and asked them to start refunding.

I called my last employee in LA, Mel, an engineer, and had her switch the site off and put a simple message on the homepage.

I felt empty. I just had to go through the motions and get this done.

I emailed our investors. They knew what was coming because I had kept them updated throughout this time, but I wanted them to know the detail of what was happening that day.

At the factory the security, lawyers and accountants arrived on site and the management team shortly after.

There were tears as I spoke to the team all together. Qun walked up to me once I had finished speaking, held both of my hands and cried.

Now it was time to let the world know what was happening. I posted to Instagram:

When we started Shoes of Prey nearly ten years ago, we had a grand vision for what the future of fashion retail might look like. We believed that women shouldn't just settle for mass-produced styles and sizes that were chosen for them. We saw a future where women around the world could design their own shoe, in their absolutely perfect size, and have it made just for them.

The early signs were great, from the local market stalls to our first global online orders; it was clear we had created something people enjoyed and appreciated. As a business we were profitable very early, and we brought on board world-class investors and advisers to help us realise our vision.

In the years that followed we tested many channels to scale what we had created. From award-winning physical stores, to wholesaling, and of course our direct to customer online experience. All the indicators for our testing were great—things like NPS, basket size and more were all positive and pointed to a healthy future. We took on more funding from intelligent, visionary investors who saw the same potential we saw, invested in R&D, and welcomed more great teammates to Shoes of Prey, along with millions of customers around the world.

We built a global community of millions of shoe-lovers, a brand, leading edge technological innovation, proprietary software, manufacturing assets, patents, and more. And most recently we began actively supporting many brands around the world, fulfilling their design needs with on-demand manufacturing.

However, just like every company, behind the scenes, we faced struggles. While all the indicators and data were positive, we were not able to truly crack mass-market adoption. We remain passionate and positive about our vision for the future of fashion retail. But we are making the difficult decision today to pause orders and actively assess all our options to either sell, or at a later date, reboot the business with substantial changes.

Everything we achieved over the last ten years is because of our awesome investors and team who have executed incredibly well to build world-class mass customisation, and pioneer this area. We will be saying goodbye to many of our wonderful teammates, and we are actively helping them transition into new positions with other companies. If you are a fellow business owner in the fashion or retail industries looking for great talent, please get in touch as we have some incredibly smart, passionate, dedicated people we can introduce you to.

We will cease normal trading to go through this process. Our customers with outstanding orders will either receive their shoes as promised, or a full refund if we have been unable to make their shoes before this pause.

Trying to create something that no-one else has done before is a wonderful mix of belief and optimism, from yourself and the visionary investors who all have a healthy risk appetite. Because of these factors, the team at Shoes of Prey had the opportunity to build incredible things. I hope that we leave a strong legacy for others to learn from and adapt, and it is our aim to be able to build on this in future as well. We were able to change the retail supply chain model, help retailers and designers reduce waste, make mass customisation real, and combat the impact of fast fashion. Shoes of Prey made huge inroads—more than any other brand—at cracking customisation at a huge scale. I will watch with great support and hope as other brands can pick up where we're leaving off for the moment.

Today is a sad moment. And I have to admit, writing this note is not where I wanted to be. It breaks my heart. Nevertheless, I will continue to share our story and more details now and into the future, so that others can learn from our experience, and I will update you when I have more news to share.

Lastly, I would like to thank everyone for their support over the past ten years and through to this current time. From our supporters in the media, to the millions of women around the world who have designed shoes with us, our great investors, advisers, friends and family. Thank you all for your continued support, and stay tuned x

The team rose

I had a massive lump in my throat and kept blinking away tears as I focused my eyes on the screen at the public message about our cessation of trade. Lily, our head of stitching, and Simon, our head of production, came to my desk.

They told me that they could see there were still shoe orders that had been started and needed to be completed. 'Don't cancel them,' they said. 'The workers want to stay to finish the orders.'

It was a Tuesday morning. With no additional pay—there was no more money—they stayed with me in the factory through till Friday afternoon to finish the orders.

My mind and heart operated separately at this point. My mind stayed the course and got done everything that needed to be done. But my heart was just lost. Who would I be without Shoes of Prey? Would I ever do anything again? Would I still have friends? What would I do everyday? Who would want me?

My family and friends stuck by me in this time. They called daily. Vuki even did a trip to China with me during one of my hellish weeks towards the very end. They reminded me, daily (and Vuki reminded me hourly) that there was light at the end of the tunnel, even if I couldn't see it now.

The process is long

Even in ceasing trading, the company was still not finished. There were deals in play in the background. The closure just held everything still, to stop us accruing debt. I was balancing so many different definitions of what the end was. Was it now? Or would it be if we didn't secure more funding? What if we sold? What if we went into liquidation? Were there any scenarios where a stakeholder had the power to make a unilateral decision on this? One moment I was mourning my emotional connection to the company I had created, the next I was wondering if there was a way for it to be turned around, or if it really was the end.

Eventually the balls I was juggling dropped—it was the end. None of the other options could be pursued. We had just one secured creditor on our books, and after many negotiations over many months, they had taken the stance (as was their right) that their security would be enforced. (A secured creditor is someone who lends you money and in exchange, you promise that they can take ownership of certain assets if you default on any terms of that loan.) Naturally, no investor wants to put money into a situation where any of it may be used to pay off creditors instead of powering the business and gaining greater value, so that was it; there were no more moves that could be made. We were dead.

The company's process of closure is ongoing as I pen this book. Even in a liquidation—which some characterise as a 'sale'—the legal process around it is not quick. And on a personal level it's challenging to continue to provide energy to something that you know is over, for such a long period after you have made your peace with it. The only reason I do is to ensure that I have created the best closing scenario for all of our stakeholders.

The support and understanding is incredible

I was terrified of my public failure in ceasing trade with Shoes of Prey and entering liquidation. I felt scared to go outside; I avoided public forums; when I did meet new people, I froze when they asked me what I do for a living.

Yet none of the interactions that did happen were vicious. None were mean. None were scathing. There were of course frustrated customers, some who I know as I write are still awaiting gift certificate refunds from our liquidators in this long process, and others in the small group of gift certificate holders I mentioned earlier who will not be able to be refunded. However in the business community, I got messages of support and complete understanding from a group of people I admired—many of whom I had never guessed would have had this type of experience in their own history. I felt in some ways welcomed to the club of entrepreneurs.

PHASE 9
ON REBOOTING

---

reboot

re·boot | \ (ˌ)rē-ˈbüt

to shut down and restart

to start anew: to make a fresh start

CHAPTER 21
WHAT I KNOW NOW

In the final chapters of Shoes of Prey, when I felt my identity, purpose and creation all falling away, all that was left was me. A blank slate. Or so I thought. As I flicked back through old diaries I used to define my personal goals, I saw that I'd actually given this so much thought; I just hadn't revisited it for a while.

Personal goals matter

Many years ago, at the Virgin Australia Melbourne Fashion Festival I was very lucky to be invited to speak on a panel with Renzo Rosso (founder of Diesel and Only the Brave), Nicola Formichetti (creative director at Diesel and stylist to Lady Gaga — remember her meat dress?) and Fern Mallis (founder of NYC Fashion Week). It was moderated by Glynis Traill-Nash (just about my favourite fashion editor).

After the session I joined the audience as representatives of the active wear brand Lululemon hosted a workshop on goal-setting. The format was simple. This is how I recall it:

1. Divide your life into three areas:

    a. wellbeing: physical health, mental health

    b. career: now and in the future

    c. relationships: significant other, family, friends

2. Plot your goals for these three areas for one year's time, five years' time, ten years' time.

I wrote furiously in the session and ran out of time far too quickly. I took the page home and spent a Saturday mapping it out properly. It felt really good to write my dreams down — and how I would get there.

Partway through the exercise I realised that there was another step I needed in order to crystallise all of this: I had to define what is important to me — my values and beliefs — for each of the three areas. I had pages of scribbled values and beliefs.

When I'd had to make my toughest decisions at Shoes of Prey, at a time when there was no map, no clear 'right' or 'wrong', I came to the realisation that I'd used my personal values and beliefs as my guide. It made my stomach strong when nothing else was — and in making each decision, I got one step further through a very confronting and challenging situation. When I encountered those old scribbles after the dust had settled (they'd been parked in the back of my bookshelf all these years), it was emotional to read over them. Not much had changed. It was comforting. I knew who I was after all. I still had my identity.

Being nice is actually a really good idea

I remember my mum telling me when I was little that 'you can't please everyone' and that 'not everyone will like you'. And I thought to myself, 'I'll show you!'

There followed years of me consciously going out of my way to be nice, being heavily influenced by those around me, and being very secretive about what I really thought ... not exactly the stereotype of the high-achieving businessperson.

While I've learned to calibrate the niceness levels depending on context, I've learned that being nice is not only okay — it comes with some significant advantages:

- *When people like you they want to champion you.* I don't think I really fully appreciated the desire we have to see people we like succeed. I should have understood it just from pop culture norms — the hero or heroine is almost always someone we really like. I know that when I have a good connection with someone I'm more likely to think of them for opportunities. I remember being at a global forum and I'd met one of the most senior people at the event earlier on.

We got on really well, and when I spoke up and added points to the formal conversation, this person would back up everything I said, which was great for credibility in a group of people I would later go on to pitch.

- *Warmth builds rapport.* No matter the status or role a person holds, we're all human. And there are some characteristics we all share: we all want to be liked and we enjoy it when someone is interested in us. When you're nice you're used to creating warmth in your conversations—smiling and giving social cues that you like the person you're talking to, asking questions to show you're interested. The rapport that comes from this often makes it easier to pick up the phone to that person with an idea or question, and, per the previous point, it predisposes them to want to help if they like you.

- *You hone your intuition.* Nice people tend to observe and listen to people a lot more than they speak themselves, which means years of learning to read between the lines, understand body language and watch for any other emotional cues. This means you have a really good read on situations that can help you to time messages or understand how a negotiation is going.

- *It increases your empathy.* When you can empathise with a person, you come closer to understanding why they behave in a certain way. This means you're well placed to understand customer needs, and handle HR issues, in a more intimate way than those with lower empathy.

If you take these strengths from being a nice person, and pair them with good business characteristics such as the ability to be firm and direct, face confrontation, and know when and how to say no, you'll see that nothing actually prevents you from being a nice person and a good businessperson. In fact, being nice makes you a *better* businessperson.

It's good — no, it's important — to care about what you do

I've read a lot of business and marketing books that tell us to look for the gap that needs filling in order to create opportunity and success. This is true. But opportunity and success also follow passion, because no-one can do better than you at something you're really, truly passionate about. In my opinion this is where great brands start—by doing, building or providing something that they genuinely and authentically believe in.

For some reason, we're really good at *not* following our passion. It's unnervingly common for me to have a conversation with someone who will say 'Oh, I absolutely love *x* but I don't have the skills/experience to pursue it'.

To me, this is a really great example of self-sabotage. There are always ways to pick up new skills. You may be busy, you may not be able to fund further study—but you can intern. You can ask for subject matter experts to meet with you so you can learn from them. In most cases, you have the internet at your fingertips to research and learn endlessly. There's always a way. And to cut off the prospect of doing something you think you might love, because you can't do it yet, is totally insane.

And, on top of all of that, people love to follow and invest in people who are genuinely passionate about what they are doing. This way you will never be 'selling'. Your pitch will be compelling because it's really something you believe in, not just something you are hawking.

You have to do everything before you're ready. That is the only way anything ever gets done.

Find out what you care about

I'm generally an impatient person who likes to see fast results from my work. (So writing a whole book was a pretty big challenge.) As I look towards my professional future, the first question I'm ruminating on is 'What do I care about?'

In many ways, I built momentum around what I cared about in the past and then it had a momentum of its own. Shoes of Prey became its own entity—larger than any one person. And I became part of that momentum. I've come to realise that you have to break momentum when you are in this kind of rhythm to come up for air, ask conscious questions, and check in. Are you still doing what you care about? Are you still building towards your personal goals? Make sure you spend a little bit of time with a blank slate to really answer those questions. And then, if the answer is something different from what you're doing now, have the courage to execute a new start.

How to beat procrastination

I never, ever in a million years imagined I'd be one of those overly muscular, tank-top-wearing Crossfit beefcakes. But I signed up after seeing a very well-targeted Facebook ad for a gym in Santa Monica that promised a female-focused six-week introduction program.

It became my antidote for anxiety, body dysmorphia and general lack of confidence. I faithfully rose at 5.30 am three times a week (well let's be honest, not every single week without fail) and found humour, relief and happiness in lifting a barbell over my head like I'd seen in the Olympics (albeit with a lot less weight, of course).

But during the final year of Shoes of Prey, there was literally no room for anything but work. Instead of going to Crossfit I began rising at 5.30 am to hit my desk, not putting my laptop down till 11 pm, day after gruelling day.

Almost a full year later, having not exercised at all during that time, I found myself back on the gym floor with a Crossfit trainer running me through a session to assess my technique and level of fitness before I jumped back into training again. I started out on the rower and felt like I was flying. My body, mind and spirit had missed this kind of exertion SO much. I pushed harder with my legs, sped up, and ... about 400 metres into the row my speed dropped like a rock. My body wasn't conditioned like it once was, and my legs were super tired already. Brow furrowed, face screwed up, my brain screaming with embarrassment and wondering what the trainer was thinking of me, I tried to push harder again. I heard over my shoulder, 'Calm down. Slow down. You'll get stronger going slower'.

I have to admit that my initial gut response was 'f*** you'. But I kept that inside and instead I listened; I slowed down. I unfurrowed my brow, unscrewed my face, stopped my brain yelling at me. And I started to enjoy the movements. I got through the workout, realised I was at square one again, and that was okay.

I would need to take this approach with everything moving forward. I'd have to find patience with this slower pace and a calmness in reconditioning myself. I would have to get very present to be able to rebuild and not procrastinate on the hard work. That feels like a tall order.

For the record, I still find myself fighting the moment, wishing I was already at the finish line, every single day. Even as I write this book, I have already written the marketing plan … before I even have a finished book to market. I struggle with the nitty-gritty. Time passes, and I think, 'Oh, I'm a day closer to the finish'—but I know that without the necessary attention and work that day, it just means that all the days left in my timeline are going to be overfull.

And that is rarely a winning strategy.

I'm a procrastinator. I find it hard to concentrate on something that's going to take multiple attempts to achieve, or a long period of time to complete. But, the simple trick I've started to play on myself is to simply enjoy what I'm doing. When I reflect on the ten years of Shoes of Prey, there truly were so many extraordinary moments. Many of which I don't think I was present enough to really appreciate.

One of the biggest game changers for me was David Allen's book *Getting Things Done*. I guess there's a reason it's a bestseller. He's got a lot of references to 'filing cabinets', 'facsimiles' and 'in-trays', which may not apply to you, but overall, the advice was amazing. These are the top tips that were game changing for me:

- *Take as much as you can out of your brain.* I didn't realise how much I was trying to keep in my brain, and I definitely didn't want to admit how unreliable my brain is in that way. I also didn't realise how much this stopped me from being able to think more clearly and strategically. Now I try to write everything down. Michael emails himself when he needs to remember something; I've stolen that technique, and it works. But it doesn't stay in my inbox as a 'to-do'.

- *Use your calendar as your to-do list, not your inbox.* The really cool thing about this is that when you get to the end of a day and feel like you got nothing done, you can look back at your calendar and see what you did get done. You can also get a really good sense of how long a piece of work takes you, by having a record of how much time you are actually spending on it. Lastly, it's a great tool for helping you to keep promises — you can see if you're going to get something done or not, and when you'll be able to get to it, much more clearly, which means you can keep everyone around you informed.

It makes you much better to work with, even if you're just working with yourself.

- *Have an awesome filing system.* Some people love colour coding (I do if it's a physical filing system; I'm obsessed with stationery), but for me I love keywording. I keep the vast majority of my work in the cloud, so with the right keywords and titles in the document, everything I need is a quick search away.

Once you've found yourself doing away with the weight of all this information distraction, you may find your inner critic popping up to prevent your progress.

Quieting your inner critic so you can ditch procrastination

Picture me in a packed yoga class. I slowly move my weight forward in my body as I stand on one leg on my yoga mat. Catching my other foot behind me in my hand, I pull it high into dancer's pose. A bead of sweat forms on my temple and as I reach my full extension of the pose I catch the other yogis in my class in my peripheral vision. I feel a twinge of smugness when I see one of my classmates wobble, and a fire of competitiveness at the rock-solid girl beside me.

Even in yoga, one of the most meditative practices you can do, my brain just won't shut up. It keeps on asking: 'Am I better? Am I worse?'

The comparison curse is hugely demotivating, yet in my experience a very common aspect of being human. It makes the assumption that everyone else is either much better or much worse than you. It's a voice of judgement that finds itself most at home in places like Instagram.

When I notice myself doing this, I think back on a couple of things:

- My accomplishments spreadsheet: incontrovertible evidence that I'm not so bad.

- Everything isn't as it seems; even some of the most famous companies don't turn a profit. We're all running our own race and, while context is helpful, comparison is not.

- The more time I spend comparing myself to others, the less time I have to work on progressing and improving. That energy must be laser focused.

Having the courage to simply try

Procrastination can often be about fear of failure. But you have to have the guts to step up and try. Put your ideas into action, and then follow them through. And repeat that, every single day. You have to be ready to reboot every morning, no matter what happened the day before.

When I'm adding up the reasons I shouldn't do something, the overwhelming recurring theme is atychiphobia. Otherwise known as fear of failure.

No-one wants to fail. There's a lot of literature out there about the importance of failure as a path to learning. And I firmly agree with it. But I'm also human. As a human I reserve a special little place of judgement for failure. I see others fail, and while I analyse the situation for learnings, I also do something else entirely different internally. I catch myself assuming that I would have made a decision that would have turned out better.

Many of us have witnessed or participated in this situation. It goes like this: let's say something doesn't go to plan at work. A project perhaps. You feel the manager or CEO *obviously sucks*. You *know* you would've made a better decision based on the *obvious* data points.

This is absolutely not helpful (even if it feels really good to say).

These thoughts can be re-framed for really excellent analysis. And absolutely should be. But the judgemental, mean and egotistical elements of this way of thinking are actually highly destructive.

For me at least, this is a reasonable part of where the fear of failure comes from. I don't ever want to be the person being talked about or thought about this way. Discussions like this build an environment of judgement where it's not worth the risk to try to build something. However, the truth is that being the person who disparages an idea or operates with the benefit of hindsight is much easier than being the original creator or the decision maker in the moment.

For me, Theodore Roosevelt said it best:

It is not the critic who counts; not the man who points out how the strong man stumbles, or where the doer of deeds could have done them better. The credit belongs to the man who is actually in the arena, whose face is marred by dust and sweat and blood; who strives valiantly; who errs, who comes short again and again, because there is no effort without error and shortcoming; but who does actually strive to do the deeds; who knows great enthusiasms, the great devotions; who spends himself in a worthy cause; who at the best knows in the end the triumph of high achievement, and who at the worst, if he fails, at least fails while daring greatly, so that his place shall never be with those cold and timid souls who neither know victory nor defeat.

This means there has to be a step forward from three parts of ourselves. We have to:

1. remove the personal judgement of those in the arena, and humbly learn from others' experiences

2. be a little less arrogant in believing we would have done better

3. have the courage to try, regardless of the outcome.

Giving yourself the freedom to imagine

You have to have the imagination and creative freedom to form your vision. Because without a vision to aim at, procrastination rules.

I believe that creative freedom is the riskiest, most challenging and enjoyable part of the whole process of building a vision. It demands that the mind roam free across a blank canvas, making marks upon the otherwise perfectly white expanse. It's rare and challenging to build from scratch. It requires you to imagine something in detail that hasn't existed before and then communicate it with others in a way that compels them to be just as excited about it as you are.

The first step I always take in this process is to ask myself a series of prompts that start with phrases like: 'Wouldn't it be cool if ...?' 'Oh my gosh, imagine if ...' or 'I wish that ...' and 'It's so annoying that ...' The reason I use these prompts is that they identify friction points that, with the right insight, could be the next awesome innovation. And, they require me to think outside of what exists right now.

I believe that the biggest challenge for adults in this process is stepping away from the expertise that we have spent so many years honing. Expertise, by nature, teaches us to analyse everything quickly through a particular lens, winnow it down and provide a very narrow set of solutions. When you are in this stage of imagination and creative freedom, this is the time to abandon your expertise and the focused analysis that it brings. It stunts creativity, which in turn prevents innovation. The best mindset to start with is simply solving the problem with your imagination, and then working backwards from there. Just don't let expertise get in the way of a good idea.

Then, naturally this tends to head down a path of questions like:

- Who would love that?

- How would they use it?

- How would they find out about it?

- How would the really established players in that industry need to be part of this, or be disrupted by it?

- What regulations affect this industry?

- What geography makes the most sense for this? What other countries would it work in, or not work in? Does that matter?

- Does it scale? How?

- How can it be monetised?

- What are the barriers to entry?

- Who do I know that would be great to talk to about this?

If you get to the end of these questions and still feel like it could work, then it's worth doing some actual research and stepping into the science phase of the process.

What I know about mass customisation now

When we launched in October 2009, we envisioned a future of being able to customise everything. Starting with shoes.

And the beginnings showed so much promise. We almost instantly found ourselves growing within a niche of people who loved designing their own shoes. They were our advocates and we grew primarily by word of mouth—more than 75 per cent of our traffic was organic. Our Net Promoter Scores were some of the highest in retail, hovering around 70, and we were able to break even within 2 months of launching the business.

Having been so successful in this niche we were curious about tackling the mass market. Did they want to design their own shoes? We surveyed our customers, and people who we wanted to be our customers. And they replied with a unanimous yes so long as we were able to satisfy four key elements:

1. Deliver their shoes within two weeks.

2. Make a simple and easy design experience.

3. Offer customisation at the same price as shoes off the shelf.

4. Make the shoes available in places that they already shopped.

We set about knocking down each one of these barriers by:

1. Raising capital from top tier venture capital firms, incredibly successful business-people turned angel investors and strategic targets like Nordstrom.

2. Building our own factory, which reduced our costs and sped up our delivery times—our final average delivery time to anywhere in the world was just 11 days, and.

3. Continually developing our user experience.

4. Entering distribution deals with David Jones and Nordstrom.

Our team went above and beyond many times with each complex task, ultimately implementing all successfully.

The market was trending towards personalisation more heavily every day. Jimmy Choo, Prada and Salvatore Ferragamo all introduced shoe customisation options. Gucci added handbag customisation.

But despite the market research, the trends, the initial customer adoption and the successful execution, the mass market simply wasn't there. While they loved the idea of designing, they didn't want to design. It was such a paralysis of choice. The mass market were excited about trends. They were excited about what designers were creating. They were emulating their favorite influencers.

And we found that even the trends weren't necessarily making good business models. You may recall that one of the items that validated our initial idea was that NIKEiD that reportedly developed their customisation business into US$100 million a year very quickly. What we didn't understand or properly consider was the context of this. It was most likely a drop in the ocean for that organization—potentially even loss-making for them to run, when looked at side-by-side with their core business.

All of this is completely rational, it's just that our research had indicated a new opportunity. But when we delivered on this opportunity, the market simply wasn't there.

We had built some incredible capabilities and there were still opportunities for them to find their fit. With further research, we pivoted into two areas: The first was for people with a shoe size outside of the usual: sizes smaller than an Australian size 5, sizes larger than a 10.5, or those in need of a width adjustment. The second was becoming the on-demand supplier of shoes for retailers, both of which I covered off in detail in chapter 18.

Each of these areas showed promise, but with our high fixed costs neither could scale quickly enough to hit break even. Those promising early signs we'd had with taking designing your own shoes to the mass market didn't prove out clearly enough within the runway we had, and we could not then raise another round of funding to continue to scale these, or to find another avenue for growth.

I'm proud of the way we worked through each challenge. We diligently collected data from our customers and from those whom we wanted to be our customers. Based on this we tested our ideas intelligently and when we found our test data to be so positive, our team went on to execute these initiatives beautifully.

There are still elements of mass-customisation and on-demand production that I love. In my mind it's financially a smarter business model for retailers and environmentally more sound—reducing the amount of stuff that is made, freighted around the world and discarded quickly. Instead, mass-customisation shifts the model to only sell what people want to buy. It's my great hope that we see a business model that can deliver on these elements and find mass market fit.

At the heart of it, changing consumer behaviour is very, very difficult, and attempting it *en mass* is even harder. Had we known this at the outset, we would have avoided raising capital, and simply built a healthy business to serve our niche.

I don't regret that we did take funding. I don't regret that we went on this journey. I don't enjoy that we failed, but then, no-one could have known the answer until we found it.

CHAPTER 22
THE REBOOT BUTTON

Until 28 August 2018 I would give speeches talking about the Shoes of Prey vision. I went to events, and when I made new friends I was 'the girl with the design your own shoe company'. Today, I am an author, newly married, and someone who says 'I don't know' when asked, 'What do you do?' or 'What will you do next?'

And that's totally okay. Because it's the truth.

Because I believe in business communities and relationships that tell the truth. Because when you tell the truth, you don't carry crazy burdens around in your mind. Because telling the truth is the best gift to yourself and to those around you who may find themselves in a similar situation. By telling the truth you can give someone the things you wish you had known. And, maybe even more importantly, you can give someone the knowledge that when they're having a shitty day that resembled something you went through, that they aren't alone. They didn't f*** up. They're just on a journey that's excruciating and exciting in equal measures.

As an alpha girl I'm definitely struggling with the change. I frequently feel restless, exhausted, under pressure, and under no pressure. When this identity change first happened, I furiously watched my way through the entire *Sopranos* television series and successfully pitched a *Wall Street Journal* writer to talk about Tony's shirts after. I washed every item of clothing I owned, stitched every hem and moth hole, wiped every surface of my apartment.

I was emotional, and I felt alone. And I just needed to feel really busy.

But after the journey I've been on, today I know for the first time in my life that I am a good CEO. I had the chance in the final stages of Shoes of Prey to act in this role at the most challenging time in the business. Nothing could have made me ready for this, other than simply doing it. And in doing this, I had to face the self-doubt and fear that had always been lurking in my stomach. But now I have evidence that even my brain cannot dispute: that I am enough. I never knew it, but what I needed to finally feel successful was confidence — and that's something that only I could give myself.

Maybe you're reading this book with the sparkle of an idea in mind that you just might pursue. Maybe you're reading it while you're in the fire of transition. Maybe you're reading it having come out the other side of something you don't quite understand just yet. Wherever you are, the only thing I can tell you that I know is that it's always better to try. It's always better to take action. You are smart enough. You are brave enough. You are *enough*. And what you will get out of any experience where you really put your dreams to work will be valuable. It may not be what you thought you'd get, but it'll be exactly what you needed, in its own way.

I still don't know exactly what's next. I hope it involves my community of friends who are like family and family who are like friends. I hope it involves having children of my own. I know it will involve my best friend Vuki, whom I married in 2019. And I know in that little flickering part of me that's almost ready to start again that it will be in fashion. I know when I find it, it will be with my new self-approval.

It will be with courage, confidence and passion that I will once again put on Florence + the Machine and reboot.

A WHOLE LOT OF THANK YOU

Vukasin (Vuki) Vujasinovic — the best human I know. Thank you for reading my manuscripts, giving me truthful and thoughtful feedback. For being my teammate, my best friend and the love of my life.

My family, in particular, Lucia, Keith, Anita and Vincenza (my mum, dad, sister and nonna respectively) for your love and support through this whole journey called life. And your patience when I was being a little crazy. I can't guarantee it won't happen again.

To my friends who are like family, and without whom I'm not sure I'd make my way through life with such joy. Thank you for being there without judgement and always with so much love: Rebecca Mok, Siobhan Way, Renee Baltov, Alena Titterton, Mat Eggins, Peta Tarlinton, Estee Clary, Noa Ries, Matt Newell, Jess Newell, Matt Love, Paron Mead, Becky Love, Steph Hill, Isha Jager and Jaime Brands.

To my co-founders for throwing everything into Shoes of Prey to make it the journey that it was, and to make the company everything it could be. In particular, to Michael Fox for the personal journey we navigated side by side with the professional, and to your wife Katrine who did the same. I'm so proud of us.

To the people who invested not only time and money, but also heart and soul, particularly when times were tough. Your wisdom, timely counsel and kindness were extraordinary.

To everyone who worked at Shoes of Prey, in any and all capacities. I'm sorry that this book doesn't mention every single one of you by name—you do all deserve to be mentioned by name but there simply weren't enough pages for all of our stories. You were truly the most courageous, intelligent, kind humans I have ever had the privilege of spending time with. Thank you for everything you taught me. Thank you for all the times you not only stepped up, but beyond.

To our customers, thank you for being such a critical part of the journey. For enjoying the experience we built, and for making me grin every time I saw you in our shoes in the street.

To my high school teacher Peter Derrett who gave shape to my young ideas and dreams. I still carry your lessons with me today and they still serve me every time I turn to them.

To Lucy Raymond, for believing there was a book in me.

To my cat ... Is it weird ... I don't care. To Hunter for all her purrs, snuggles and presence in truly dark moments when no one else could be there.

And if you don't find yourself listed here, just know that it wasn't by design but by mistake. Let me take you for a cup of tea to apologise and catch up.

And one very important post script, added at the very last minute to the very last proof of this book before printing ... to our unborn child. I cannot wait to meet you and share this crazy, insane, wonderful world with you.

APPENDIX A

VALUES DOCUMENT

We divided our document into three areas:

1. vision
2. values
3. culture.

Our first vision was 'Every woman can have the perfect pair of shoes'.

Our first values were:

- Passionately create happiness.
- Our primary goal is to make our customers and each other happy.
- We do work that challenges us, helps us master new skills, and makes the people around us happy.
- We all create an environment where we 'want to' come to work rather than 'have to' come to work.
- We're passionate about the work we do, and we celebrate wins.
- We should prefer decisions that maximise happiness (e.g. refunding with a smile, even if the customer is difficult, but politely firing customers who consistently behave poorly).

We explained a little more what we meant by our concept of 'passionately creating happiness':

- Creating lasting happiness is really difficult, and is hard work.
- Superficial happiness isn't happiness.

And we defined how we as a team would execute on this:

- Laziness doesn't create happiness. Selflessness does.

- The people around us can make us happy (or unhappy), but we also have the responsibility of making ourselves happy.

- The single most important thing to creating happiness is a positive attitude.

We defined what constituted constructive, thoughtful communication:

- We don't complain about problems, we brainstorm solutions.

- We all know how to use Google, but we're not shy about asking for help when we're really stuck too.

- If we're curious and something hasn't been communicated, we ask.

- We're respectful of each other's time. For example, we turn up to meetings on time and communicate appropriately for the situation (e.g. don't call a meeting if an email will suffice).

And again, we defined how we as a team would execute on this. We defined our opportunities to communicate:

- weekly one on ones (catch-ups with their manager)

- Monday lunch-time catch-ups (through the entire life of Shoes of Prey we always had lunch tables big enough to seat the whole team. It was never mandatory to eat all together, yet it was only on the rare occasion that a team member missed having lunch with us)

- quarterly financial updates

- daily huddle.

We broke down how to make a big impact:

- 20 per cent trying new things (innovation) and analysing the impact (e.g. build a new website feature, analyse the impact)

- 80 per cent amplifying what we know works (e.g. adding new shoe designs and materials, replying to customers quickly)

- we get things done with what we have; we're scrappy and quick to learn from mistakes

- we inspire each other with our thirst for excellence

- it's better to ask for forgiveness than ask for permission—we're proactive and think like business owners
- the kind of person who will succeed at Shoes of Prey is a person who, after spotting a problem, takes time from their busy schedule to ensure it gets fixed.

Our first culture points were:

- Amazing colleagues
    - as a team we hire people who inspire us and live our values
    - we won't tolerate mediocre performance or brilliant jerks
    - we're a professional sports team AND a family
    - litmus test for managers to apply to reports when thinking about development 'Which of my reports, if they told me they were leaving for a competitor, would I fight hard to keep?'
    - Employee Net Promoter Score and 360-degree feedback
- Recognise great work
    - we all publicly acknowledge when we see someone else do a great job
    - we celebrate our wins and successes!
    - great work is the output achieved rather than the hours worked
    - career development is linked to great work
- Promotion and development
    - we value colleagues who pursue self-improvement and development
    - we aid in developing people by providing the opportunity to work on new, challenging tasks
    - to be promoted the new role must be large enough to be a full-time role
    - to be promoted, we must excel in our current roles and have proven we can perform the new role

- Freedom and responsibility
  - we all thrive on freedom and are worthy of freedom
  - to an extent compatible with our roles, we're all free to manage our own hours and location of work
  - we all take responsibility to ensure customers are happy (e.g. we aim not to miss customer calls)
  - we all take responsibility to ensure effective communication between the team (e.g. everyone attends our daily huddle). We take responsibility for how our hours affect the team and make sure we are there for important meetings, meetings that need to be face-to-face and customers
- Embrace chaos
  - funding can take forever to close ...
  - resources are finite ...
  - there are never enough hours in the day ...
  - things break ...
  - there are many tasks that are no-one's job and everyone's job ...
  - we all need to be positive in the face of chaos, but also pitch in to help each other minimise chaos
- Work–life balance
  - we love coming to work, but we don't live there
  - a refreshed colleague is a productive and inspired colleague
  - we take leave responsibly; we don't hold out and spread germs, we get better fast
  - we enjoy coming to work; it's a fun, inspiring place full of people we enjoy spending time with
  - working at Shoes of Prey helps us achieve our career and life goals
  - we're not beholden to our work
  - we aim for a balance between all the fantastic parts of our life—work, family and personal.

While this was in stark contrast to another like document that we loved, the Nordstrom employee handbook, which simply said 'Use good judgement in all situations', we felt that this longer document was necessary to truly capture and define Shoes of Prey at this very young, developmental stage of our business.

Appendix B

Moving Checklist

Before you go

√	Action Item
	If you are currently renting: give sufficient notice to your landlord that you are going to move out. You may not want to give too much notice though, in case they want to start inspections immediately. Action item: read your lease and create a diary entry to give notice.
	Start selling or donating personal belongings you don't want to take with you. We may organise a joint garage sale here at the office closer to May … they are fun!
	If your Australian passport will expire soon (the next two years?), consider renewing it for as long as possible. Do this before you apply for your US visa.
	Renew your Australian drivers licence for as long as possible. You can use your AU licence to legally drive in the US (see below). Note: You can only renew your licence within 6 months of expiry. If you are within 6 months of expiry, there is a Services NSW on Rawson Place next to Central that opens at 7 am and was dead empty when last visited. If you are not within 6 months expiry, don't stress—they said that you will be able to do it all online within the next few months and get it delivered directly to you overseas.
	Obtain your E3 visa. We will help you with this.

	Get your flights booked.
	Suspend [Don't cancel!] your AU private health insurance as of the date of your departure. This will make it easy to reactivate it at a later date, without having to restart all the waiting periods.
	Cancel any gym memberships, or other subscriptions. You may need to give one or two months' notice, so check your contracts.
	Ensure we've either already set up US health insurance for you in the US, or that you have appropriate travel insurance for the first few weeks when you arrive. A short stint in a US hospital can cost an arm or a leg—literally!
	If you already maintain life insurance, or any other kind of insurance, you'll need to research the implications of moving to the US.
	Make sure you've wrapped things up at Sydney HQ, which means making sure your station and any belongings (including in the warehouse) have either been packed appropriately or disposed of, and you have properly handed over any tasks you won't be able to do once gone.
	Box up any belongings that can be ocean-freighted. Note, these may not arrive in the US until late June-ish. You can store things in the office warehouse in the meantime provided everything is kept neat and tidy. Please ensure all boxes are labelled clearly—in big letters—with your name, and the contents of the box. e.g. 'Box 1 of 5, Joe Bloggs, Kitchenware, FRAGILE'. While reasonable care will be taken, moving things is at your own risk, so please ensure things are appropriately packaged to prevent damage during transit. When you're done, print out a complete inventory of your boxes (including the contents of each) and hand to Dave. Be sure to note any hazardous or potentially risky items (e.g. anything flammable, or potentially restricted from import, e.g. plants, seed, nuts, drugs, your grandma, weapons, etc. ... you know the drill!).
	Note: the shipping company will likely need to open all your boxes and re-pack everything. They need to do this to ensure that no contraband is shipped, and also to ensure that the shipment is covered by insurance.

	Obtain advice on the implications of the move on your particular tax situation. BDO has a handy guide (called 'Leaving Australia – Tax Guide') that will give you an overview, for example, of Capital Gains Tax scenarios that may arise if you own a house or other property.
	Make a list of all institutions/organisations you deal with, and update all of your mailing addresses with them [tip: try to use an AU friend or family address, ideally someone who you trust to open your mail for you.] Don't forget: • Banks • Medicare • Private health insurance provider • Doctor/dentist • Department of Transport • ATO • Your super fund • Frequent flyer or loyalty programs • Alumni associations (university, high school) • Electricity, gas providers • Internet provider • Phone. You may want to consider purchasing a temporary redirect service from Australia Post for a number of months to ensure you've changed over all addresses. I recommend starting this process as soon as possible.
	Research which US bank you wish to use so that you're ready to sign up immediately when you arrive—as an interim it might be useful to sign up for the Citibank card that makes international transfers easy and is low on international fees: https://www.citibank.com.au/aus/banking/everyday_banking/citibank_plus.htm

	Increase the credit limit on your local AU credit cards if possible. You won't be able to get a US credit card until you build a US credit score. This may take a number of years to achieve.
	Notify your AU bank/credit card providers that you will be overseas, so that they don't block your cards once you try to use them in the US.
	If you wish to keep your AU mobile number, sign up for the cheapest monthly plan or prepaid service you can find. Record a message on your voicemail telling people you no longer check the account, and refer them to your email address instead. Warning: Keep in mind a lot of AU banks (and now even Google sometimes) require you to enter an SMS code to transfer money or update your account, so be careful cancelling your phone number entirely! This may be difficult to fix if you're in the US and need to do an immediate transfer. You may want to consider using an obliging family member's mobile number instead.
	You may wish to consider giving 'power of attorney' (the right to execute documents as if they are you) to a trusted family member.
	Obtain copies of all important documents, e.g. your passport, birth certificate, driver's licence and US visa sticker, and keep them in a safe place, e.g. Google Drive.
	Pack! HINT 1: Ideally bring possessions you can't afford to re-purchase or sentimentally replace. Most items (crockery, white goods, bedding, etc.) can be purchased fairly cheaply. HINT 2: There may be some useful items you may not think to pack including universal adaptors.

	If you are renting: depending on when you move out, you may need to coordinate with a local friend who can be there to meet the landlord if they require that for the final inspection. Arrange for the final inspection and drop-off of keys. To save you the hassle, you may want to arrange for a cleaner to do your final cleaning (Todd has a good reference for a cleaner). Fill out your NSW Fair Trading Claim for Refund of Bond Money form and send to your leasing agent. Cancel or transfer-over your utilities to your leasing company or the next tenant.
	Install Uber and Lyft on your phone—these make travelling around easy, fun, safe and relatively affordable.
	Read up on US language differences.
	Organise a wicked going away party!

Once you arrive

√	Action Item
	As soon as you arrive: Sign up for a cell (mobile phone) plan.
	At least 10 days after arriving, and good to do asap, apply for a US Social Security Number. Details here: http://www.ssa.gov/pubs/EN-05-10096.pdf Note that if you choose to take the I-94 form as one of the proof documents, a print out of the online form is enough.
	As soon as you have your Social Security Number, open a bank account. At the very least you'll want a chequing account with debit card access. Everyone writes cheques for things like rent in the US. It's very cute! [People will get all weird if you ask them for their bank account details to transfer them $20. It's not the done thing.]

Apply for a credit card to start building a credit rating. The best card to apply for when you don't have a credit rating is at Capital One and it is called a secured Mastercard.

To apply, you will need:

- A Social Security Number

- An address for correspondence to be sent to. You don't have to live there or prove that you do.

- A savings account to pay the application fee of $49 USD (Your Australian account is sufficient, however you will need to know what your bank's ABA Routing Number is. You can Google it. For ANZ, it is 021000021).

- You can apply for it online. The card will have a very low limit ($300-500 USD) but make sure you use it and pay it off on time every month—this pattern is what builds your credit rating. A good idea may be to have your mobile phone billed to it and then set up an auto payment from your savings account each month so you can set and forget.

Note that it will take about a month for your credit card to arrive. And, you can customise your card (who wouldn't!!)

First month: Secure a letter of recommendation from Shoes of Prey to help with securing an apartment.

Create a 'portfolio' to take to viewings, with references, etc. ready to hand to the real estate agents. Your portfolio should include the following documents (check this list with your agent before you start applying, sometimes you don't need all these documents):

- photo ID

- your employment letter

- your last 3 bank statements

- your last 2 tax returns

- your last 2 pay slips

	• any asset documentation • your contact information • optional are reference letters from past landlords and others.
	Find your new apartment or house!!
	Once you have a permanent residential address, get a: 1. California ID card—recommended; otherwise you'll need to bring your passport to bars and clubs, which is terribly lame and inconvenient, or a 2. California driver's licence—optional; remember you can continue to use your AU licence for as long as it is valid and you're not a 'California resident'.
	Register your new US contact details with the Australian Department of Foreign Affairs and Trade (optional).
	Register as an overseas voter, or unenroll completely from the Australian electoral roll; the choice is yours, depending on how much you love voting.
	If you have savings in Australia that generate interest income, notify your Australian banks that you have moved overseas, so that they can update your tax residency status. They will then start automatically collecting the 'non-resident withholding tax' (10%). In years where this is your only income in Australia, you may not need to file an AU tax return.
	You will also need to inform all AU banks that you are now a resident of the US for tax purposes. This will mean your AU bank (via the ATO) will need to undertake certain reporting to the US Government. See, for example, ING's declaration form.
	Lodge an early tax return with the ATO for the 2014/2015 tax year. You should get advice from your accountant on your particular circumstances, including any Capital Gains Tax.

	Locate a suitable US tax accountant. You will need to file your first US tax return in early 2016. If you have more than $10 000 in foreign bank accounts, you will need to declare this to the IRS as well. You may want to use someone like H&R Block, who have offices in AU and the US so should be able to help you navigate the cross-border tax implications.
	Locate a suitable primary care physician in your neighbourhood and check they are accepting new patients. This is good to do before you get sick and need immediate care.
	Sit back and enjoy all of the wonderful things living in the US provides: Hulu.com, Mexican food and Las Vegas, to name a few!!

Appendix C

FUNDRAISING

Define your strategy

When deciding whether to raise capital, the first question we asked ourselves was, 'What kind of business are we building? Lifestyle or behemoth?'

Lifestyle businesses are great. When I say 'lifestyle', I mean building a company that will allow you to work for yourself and make some great money to allow you to live comfortably both financially and in terms of the hours you do. Lifestyle businesses can change over time into behemoths.

Generally speaking, if you're building a lifestyle business you'll probably need some initial capital that you pay back (maybe a bank loan, or perhaps a loan from friends and family) but then once you've paid that off, you focus on being profitable and don't need to continually top up the cash reserves with loans or other types of funding.

Behemoths are more about building something large, quickly. If you can show that:

- you want to build a behemoth
- you can acquire a customer for much less than their lifetime value (lifetime value is the number you get when you count how much the customer spends in their total number of purchases from you after you acquired them)
- you have a great team with a solid plan on how to do this

then you can probably build a big business with some investment up front.

If you're considering venture capital as the way you'd like to get investment, this is only going to be interesting to them if you are planning to grow the business into something large (let's say a business worth over $100 million).

One way to think about venture capital is like strapping a rocket to your back. It gives you the power (cash) to hire more people and spend more on sales and marketing so you can grow the business much faster. But the tradeoff is more risk. If you don't get the growth you expect there is a much higher chance of running out of capital and destroying your fragile business.

The next issue we considered was accountability. We loved not having to report to anyone and being agile. But we were ambitious about making Shoes of Prey a behemoth. We felt confident we could be accountable with the right kind of 'boss', so we decided raising venture capital was the way to go.

Decide how much money to raise

In our experience there were four main factors that needed to be weighed up to decide this. They were:

1. What would we spend the money on?
    And how far can we get with the money? Can it last for at least 18 months and is that long enough and enough money to get us to the next big milestone that will allow us to raise more capital (or be breakeven)

2. What stage of the company are we at?

3. What is our valuation?

4. How much of the company do we want to give away?

1. What would you spend the money on?

Knowing what you'd spend the money on determines how much money you need and when you expect to have not only made it back, but also made a healthy return for your investors. I'll talk more about what a healthy return is below. Remember in the funding chapter, I outlined some of these as hiring people, equipment, marketing and addressing consumer data.

2. What stage of the company are you at?

When you raise capital, your company will normally fall into a classification that is shorthand for investors to understand. They want to hear in broad brushstrokes, what your company has achieved so far, and what it would spend money on to move to the next stage of growth. I'll map out the first two stages, because after that you're likely to know this game very well!

Seed stage

This is when you've got your idea, you have a plan to make it work and a strong team ready to execute it when you get an injection of capital. You may have already built your Minimum Viable Product (discussed in chapter 2) and have tested it on some people. In the past the majority of these companies were not making revenue, but today it's increasingly common for this class to have some revenue. If you are making revenue at this stage, you have more leverage to get a better valuation. The best people to approach at this stage are friends and family, incubators, angel investors, government grants, competitions for new ideas and venture capital firms who invest at seed stage.

Series A

This is when you've got your idea off the ground, proven that it works, have a strong dedicated team, customers who have purchased multiple times from you, a plan to make it grow and a hypothesis that there is a big market out there for your idea. At this stage, you can include institutional investors, a wider group of venture capital firms and family offices (which are wealth management advisory firms for ultra high net worth individuals).

However, there are frequent shifts of opinion on what really constitutes a 'seed', 'series A' or other stage of company investment. That's because each stage often has an amount the industry expects you to raise at that level and a related valuation. Both of these change depending on the market, industry and investment trends. And, while they are generally agreed upon at any given time, there's certainly nothing set in stone.

3. What is your valuation?

First I would recommend looking at other companies in your industry who have raised funding and how they were valued at your stage. You can draw likenesses with your vision and their success to boost your valuation.

There are industry rules of thumb for starting valuations at each stage — Seed, Series A, and so on. These change according to the business cycle and depending on what areas are popular with investors. You should seek out and ask other founders who have raised capital recently to get a feel for these valuation ranges.

Sometimes there are also general industry calculations you can use to think about where your valuation might start. It's often your annual revenue multiplied by an expected or approximate industry multiple. For example, in software, that might be a multiple of 10 times your revenue, and in retail it might be more like 3 or 4. It's worth doing some research as to whether there is an accepted multiple in the industry you are in and how it is currently applied. Don't forget to look for outliers to this, and the reasons that they have raised more than the calculations, or, why they might have taken less.

4. How much of the company do you want to give away?

The general wisdom shared with us on this topic is that 'it's better to own a small slice of a big pie than a large slice of a small pie'. But in your first raise, in particular, it's worth thinking carefully about whether you want to give away a controlling stake of your company.

When I spoke about this question with one of my favorite Venture Capitalists, Rick Baker, a founding partner of Blackbird Ventures, he said

> I would go so far as to say you should be careful NOT to give away a stake that would see the founder group lose control for at least the seed and series A rounds ... founders should absolutely guard their equity and think hard about giving away every percentage point of equity as it goes faster than you think, especially as you need to raise larger and larger amounts as you scale an even highly successful business.

And he's right. Your percentage ownership of the company will dilute with every subsequent raise you make, so to lose a controlling stake in your first raise will significantly diminish your ability to really determine the direction of the company, particularly if you find yourself in a hostile situation.

If you do raise funding, you may be wondering whether it's alright for you to sell some of your equity to the new investors so that you can take some cash off the table. After all, you've probably already taken a lot of risk and not yet given yourself a return.

Generally speaking, it's not well received to table this discussion at seed or series A rounds of funding. That's because the risk is still extremely high, and investors want to see every dollar they invest in you and the company put to work on making this company grow fast. When you get to series B and/or your business is making material revenues, that's the time to put the item on the agenda for discussion. And, for what it's worth, I would even recommend taking a small amount of cash off the table at each of the *later* raises you do from Series B onwards. At this later stage it can align investor and founder interests to do so. If the founders have been able to take enough money off the table to buy a house, for example, it allows them to separate the financial interests of the company from their own financial needs and be more comfortable to aim for a massive outcome, even though that's riskier.

Don't be afraid to bring this up when the company is in the right position for you to do so. But make sure you address it in a way so that it doesn't become a point of contention in closing the deal.

Consider the reasons not to do it

There's no such thing as a free lunch. If you can't see your company being able to commit to achieving the numbers you'd need in order to entice investors, or your business is growing sustainably and in line with what you had aimed for, then it's not worth signing up to a new set of complexities that may, particularly in the former scenario, ultimately sink your business.

Think about salaries

We didn't take salaries from the business until we were funded. And even then, from that day through till the end of the business, we didn't pay ourselves market value. There were even tough times in the business where we cut our lower-than- market value salaries by 50 per cent. We took the view that it was better to have the liquidity in the business and that our salaries were cushioned by the large shareholdings we each had as founders.

In my view, it's entirely reasonable to make sure the founders do have comfortable salaries. As investors, you want the founders to be worried about growing the business and fully focused on that, not worrying about whether they can pay their rent.

Whenever we discussed salary with our board, we always presented it as a case, as you would with any other expenditure that requires board approval. We would speak over:

- any market information we were able to collect on founder salaries at a similar stage
- information connected to cost of living that made sense to share
- our performance as a company.

This gave us a dispassionate, rational way to have the discussion.

Decide which type of investors to target

There are many different kinds of investors; here are just a few:

- friends and family
- angel investors
- venture capitalists
- incubators
- grants
- competitions
- private equity
- institutional investors
- family offices
- banks.

My experience is largely with venture capital, so I'll speak to this in more detail. But first I'll also discuss two other common types: friends and family, and angel investors.

Friends and family

We did take a small amount of 'friends and family' money during Shoes of Prey. The learnings on this are many:

- Investments like these have absolutely no guarantee of returns; they are very high risk. Any money invested should be money that friends and family are comfortable to lose (and that you'd be comfortable with them losing).

- Manage expectations on how frequently you plan to communicate with your friends and family investors, and to what level of detail. There are normally information rights attached to shareholdings — if a person falls under a certain percentage, it can mean that they have no right to any information at all. And, especially at the early stages, it's a lot of work to provide updates frequently while still getting the work done that will give their investment the best chance of success. In any case, it's best to manage this communication cadence and level of detail up front.

- Be prepared for this to potentially affect your personal relationship, and take this into account when considering going out to family and friends — particularly if they have not previously made investments like this.

As you can see the trickiest part of this kind of funding isn't the cash itself; it's the personal relationship. The complexity and emotional weight this can add is significant, and should not be underestimated if you do decide to take this form of funding.

Angel investors

Angel investors are typically wealthy individuals who are sophisticated investors—which means they have enough experience and market insight to be considered almost professional investors for themselves. In some countries (I'm especially thinking of Australia) there are specific legal definitions for what constitutes a sophisticated investor.

The time that you may be most likely to look to angel investors for funding is when you are still proving that your idea will really work.

While angel investors are a step more professional than friends and family, they do sit neatly in a place where they are generally managing all of their own decisions, on their own money. They often invest based on trust and gut feel, whereas venture capital firms normally do more due diligence. Therefore angel investors are frequently being able to move more quickly than some other funding options.

That being said, angels do tend to have a more conservative approach to what they will fund, because generally speaking they have less of an opportunity to build a portfolio of risks.

The most important thing to remember if you want to raise from angel investors is that you need to earn their trust.

Venture capital

Most venture capital firms will have a carefully honed mandate on what and how they invest. It will cover:

- the industries in which they invest
- what they look for in founders and management teams
- how long they have to invest the money in their fund
- the percentage of the startup company they will take
- the stages at which they'll invest
- how much money they like to invest
- the time frame by when they expect to see a return (for example, five years? Ten years?)
- what type of return they hope to see (this can depend on a multiple of revenue among other factors)
- what kind of liquidation preference they will get (a liquidation preference means, in the event of the company having to liquidate, what rank they have amongst creditors to be paid any proceeds).

These mandates are so important, and they're not often broken because these are the promises on which they have agreed with their investors that they will invest their capital.

The best place I have found to understand all of this, and get the right contact details for venture capitalists, is through talking to entrepreneurs who have recently raised, and some good old-fashioned networking. Founders are normally really happy to share their experiences, and given that the investment landscape is always evolving, they should have some of the most relevant and accurate information to share with you. If you're targeting a particular investor, it's also worth reaching out to an entrepreneur they've already invested in to learn about their approach, and to ask for an introduction. If you already have investors in your company, they can also be a good source of this information and introductions to additional investors.

And, if you're looking for background reading, another source I found really helpful was Pitchbook, a subscription-only database of investors, investments and industry overviews.

Make the call

The pitch

Pitching to investors comes in many forms. We pitched in boardrooms, pool cabins, nightclubs and cafés. We talked to billionaires, tyre kickers, CEOs and friends. While each person has a slightly different idea of exactly the information that they would like to hear, there are generally some principles that stay the same.

Up front, what's the idea

Be clear, be concise and state the idea up front. A really excellent banker I had the privilege of working with passed on the age-old wisdom that when pitching:

1. Tell them what you're going to tell them.

2. Then tell them.

3. Then summarise what you told them.

So, following these rules, tell them in one *very* short sentence what the idea is.

Then you can tell them why it's the answer to a problem. Show how that problem manifests. Make it relevant to them. Then you loop back to what the idea is.

I was also told that a great structure to think of is to have your audience agree with a series of assertions you make, so that when you tell them your company is the answer, they say 'of course'. This is compelling because you take them on a journey that allows them to have the same realisation that you did in starting the company. I like to think of this approach as 'yes, yes, yes, of course'.

What's the blue sky?

What could your business become if you were to chase your wildest dreams? What's the industry you're disrupting? Have some numbers, such as the size of the addressable market, to back you up. The way you might do this is by answering questions such as: Where are the customers? How many of them are there? How much money will they give you over the course of their lifetime? What will it take to get them to make their first purchase with you?

These are largely marketing focused questions, but they are of huge importance to proving that the audience exists, that it's large and that your company is capable of both acquiring and repeat selling to them. The funding chapter offers the most practical ways that we used to approach this.

Show the unit economics

Unit economics are the costs and revenues of a business on a per unit basis. For Shoes of Prey, a unit was a pair of shoes. Unit economics is a simple way to understand whether a business can be successful—and, if not, what would need to change to make it successful. Within this, some very basic metrics to consider, in addition to the Cost Of Goods Sold (COGS, covered in chapter 6; that is, if you sell a physical product) are Life Time Value (LTV—how much a customer will spend with you over the duration of their life) and Customer Acquisition Cost (CAC—how much you pay in marketing activity to get someone to make their first purchase). As long as the LTV is bigger than the CAC, there's a chance of success. (But obviously, the higher the LTV the better.)

From here, you need to know everything there is to know about how your business operates and how your customers behave. Your deck should have two slides on numbers: one slide showing historical information (unless you're pre-launch) and one slide with projections.

Who is the team?

It's often said that venture capitalists invest in people. And I really believe this. In our pitches we always started by introducing ourselves and our backgrounds. And if one of us couldn't be present, we spoke about them on their behalf. The key points we covered off.

Your team should include people who can each offer a different way of doing things, and ideally cover all of the main functions of the business. For example, with the three of us at Shoes of Prey, we had IT, operations and branding covered initially, which are each very important parts of the business.

Be polished

Perhaps the best way the venture capitalist (VC) can make a call on you is by seeing how polished you are in the pitch. This is one time that you really need to be able to answer every question then and there. You personally are one of the most important aspects of the pitch; VCs want to understand that you as a founder are going to be able to execute well and make this company a success.

Keep up the momentum

When you've done the pitch, you have to keep up the momentum. VCs are time poor and hear a lot of pitches. Reply to them quickly to keep momentum up on your discussions and stay front of mind.

Make your pitch deck easy to read and easy to share

Generally speaking, your deck should be no more than 15 slides (though you can add as much additional information as you like to an appendix). Each slide should be drafted to make one key point. I'd recommend checking out Vinod Khosla's video 'Pitch the way VCs think: Presenting PowerPoint with Emotion'. His firm, Khosla Ventures, was one of our major investors, and the video provides an excellent overview on how to pitch VCs.

Make it easy to share by hosting it on a platform like Google Docs or Dropbox. You can adjust the share settings to ensure you understand who has access to it and how they can access it. It will be up to your own level of comfort to decide how concerned you are about this getting into hands you'd prefer it didn't, versus being easy for potential financiers to view.

Remember that VCs are human (!)

They make emotional decisions like any human being. The key emotion you want to tap into is the fear of missing out on an opportunity, a.k.a. FOMO. You want them to feel that this is a company that's going to make them money, and you want them to be scared of missing out. We saw this play out time and time again in our fundraising.

Once you've done the legwork and have a couple of VCs giving you term sheets (which is a short document that outlines the offer of investment), this emotion kicks in from everyone else and you'll find yourself with more people wanting to invest than you have room for. So work hard to get those first few term sheets.

***

There are a lot of great resources available to ensure you have honed your pitch to give you the best opportunity to raise the money you're after. And this is a constantly evolving space. So if you're reading this and getting ready to raise money, go beyond this book to see if you can get tips from companies that have successfully pitched the funds you're meeting, read articles written by current fund partners, and just generally get out there and research.

INDEX

Throughout the index, JF indicates Jodie Fox; SoP indicates Shoes of Prey